RYAN ADAMS

Michael Heatley

RYAN ADAMS

Michael Heatley

OMNIBUS PRESS

Picture research by Dave Brolan.

ISBN 0.7119.9435.8
Order No. OP 49049

Exclusive Distributors:
Music Sales Limited
8/9 Frith Street, London W1D 3JB, UK.

Music Sales Corporation
257 Park Avenue South, New York, NY 10010, USA.

Macmillan Distribution Services
53 Park West Drive, Derrimut, Vic 3030, Australia.

To the Music Trade only:
Music Sales Limited
8/9 Frith Street, London W1D 3JB, UK.

Every effort has been made to trace the copyright holders of the photographs in this book but one or two were unreachable. We would be grateful if the photographers concerned would contact us.

Printed in Great Britain by
Creative Print & Design, Wales.

A catalogue record for this book is available from the British Library.

Visit Omnibus Press on the web at
www.omnibuspress.com

Introduction

ONLY ONE LETTER differentiates Bryan Adams, the Groover from Vancouver, from alt.country superstar Ryan Adams. Hence the possibly apocryphal tale, told by a letter writer to *Mojo* magazine, of the man who came to see Ryan Adams at Sheffield's Boardwalk club because he thought he was a Bryan Adams tribute act . . . and came away converted.

But while the younger man from Jacksonville, North Carolina – 28 at the time of writing – has yet to write his own 'Everything I Do' (actually, he has, though not in sales terms), he already had four albums to his name before *Gold* broke it all wide open in late 2001. The Rolling Stones, Gram Parsons, Van Morrison and Neil Young have all been quoted as Adams' influences, and such lofty comparisons seem only to have stoked the fires of mythology.

Yet it could be that Steve Earle offers a more relevant comparison. A decade earlier, Earle had emerged from country to place one foot firmly in the rock arena, with earth-shaking effect. Adams' *Copperhead Road* may well be to come, but interestingly he's being pitched by management and record company to a young, trendy audience. Add fans of Young, Parsons, Morrison etc. and, even, those to whom Adams fan Elton John is king and you have a potential across-the-board audience.

But what of Adams himself? To many, he's a walking, talking contradiction, and that's something he's happy to play along with if not play up. His romances with the famous have seen him become gossip-column fodder, and while he's an expert at mesmerising an audience with the aid of a guitar, a harmonica and a book of lyrics he's taken to stadium-rocking in mini-Springsteen fashion.

The fact remains, though, that his rise has been meteoric. His début solo London gig in 2000 drew an audience of 275; in the spring of 2001 he returned to play two nights at a 500-capacity theatre, while his third visit in less than a year saw him sell out the 2,000-seat Shepherds Bush Empire. But that is where many so-called alt.country acts like Wilco, Steve Earle and the Jayhawks have levelled out.

Since then, he's moved on up both in concert status and critical standing, ensuring that the man whose breakthrough band Whiskeytown were labelled 'the Nirvana of alt.country' would not go down with the genre. Newsworthy both on and off stage, this North Carolina native had removed all room for confusion and made a name for himself as the brightest hope in American rock for the first years of a new millennium. Bryan *who*?

This will undoubtedly not be the last book on Ryan Adams, but to this writer's knowledge it is the first. I'd like to thank all those, credited or otherwise, who assisted me in the endeavour – not to mention the excellent websites which are listed in the discography. There are as many different viewpoints on his music as there are influences on Adams' work, and hopefully they've all come together to entertain and inform. He's certainly packed a lot of life and music into his first 28 years, and there's no doubt more to come.

1

The Alt.country Phenomenon

CAN THERE BE a more predictable musical genre than country? One of many jokes suggesting a negative answer runs like this: "What happens when you play a country music record backwards? You get your wife back, your house back, your truck back, your dog back . . ."

Yet it doesn't – and hasn't – always been that way. The genre most famously imbued with rock'n'roll excitement by Gram Parsons in the late Sixties has provided a more recent generation of US singers and songwriters with a means of escape from the post-punk dead end. Among those was Whiskeytown, led by Ryan Adams. Yet though he's emerged as a leading light in a genre that has variously worn the names country-rock, alt.country and Americana, he's in no hurry to be pigeonholed.

"I don't really worry about the Americana tag," he commented while still at the head of Whiskeytown. "I just think they mean bands that write songs. If you write songs and they make sense, you end up getting called Americana." As for 'alt.country', "I just would *hate* to be part of a genre in which the band would die when the genre dies, like grunge (Nirvana). Quite frankly, our biggest influences are the Stones and Fleetwood Mac, neither of which is very 'alternative' or 'country'.

"I would never diss country," he concluded. "In fact we write the best country songs. But we're just an American rock'n'roll band. That just about sums up everything we do."

The emotional content of country music has long been a target for rock bands keen to increase their musical vocabulary. A seismic shift in American music had occurred when the Grateful Dead followed in the footsteps of Bob Dylan and 'went country' in the late Sixties with the likes of *American Beauty* and *Workingman's Dead*. The Rolling Stones caught the drift with Gram Parsons' help, with songs like 'Wild Horses' (recorded both by them and Parsons' Flying Burrito Brothers) and 'Sweet Virginia', from *Exile On Main Street*, resulting.

Gram Parsons is not only the biggest single influence Ryan Adams has name-checked over the years but the man history sees as the main progenitor of country-rock. Having cut his teeth with the International Submarine Band, he joined The Byrds for 1968's seminal *Sweetheart Of The Rodeo* album before jumping ship to found the Burritos after a leadership tussle with Roger McGuinn. Far from wanting to pursue a strategy of merging country and rock, McGuinn had no idea who he'd hired: "When I hired Gram I thought he was a jazz pianist: I had no idea he'd be this Hank Williams character."

Yet as Chris Hillman, who left The Byrds at the same time as Parsons, points out, country and rock had long been bedfellows. "Elvis, when he was at Sun Records, when he was good, the initial stuff he did for Sam Phillips, that was country-rock. Country-rock, rockabilly, it's all the same thing. After he went in the army, it was over."

With the arrival of The Beatles, much of what was deemed country music seemed designed for older folks disenfranchised by the beat group phenomenon sweeping the States. Yet if you looked beneath the surface, the relationship remained: the Fab Four themselves covered songs by Carl Perkins ('Matchbox', 'Honey Don't') and Buck Owens ('Act Naturally'), as well as imparting a country flavour to the occasional Lennon-McCartney composition like 'What Goes On'. They also inherited and progressed the work of The Everly Brothers, whose harmonies were among the first to coat country with a radio-friendly sheen.

The mainstream and country music remained on separate, parallel courses, though The Byrds had done their best to bring them together. Chris Hillman, a former bluegrass mandolin player who picked up the electric bass when he joined the group, points to the presence of Porter Wagoner's 'Satisfied Mind' on their second album in 1965 as early evidence, and cites the following year's 'Time Between' as the first country-rock record. "The Byrds set the tone, and The Flying Burrito Brothers did it." That said, the 'new wave' was poorly received by the country establishment: The Byrds' gig at the Grand Ole Opry in Nashville met with a very poor reception, despite the recruitment of pedal steel player Jay Dee Manness. Both commercially and in terms of finding open minds, country-rock would look to a younger, long-haired rock audience for acceptance.

Meanwhile Bob Dylan had recruited some heavyweight help to produce his *Nashville Skyline* album, hanging round Music City long enough to record a whole (as yet unreleased) extra album with Johnny Cash. Another musician with a bluegrass background, Jerry Garcia, added his pedal steel to Crosby Stills & Nash's 'Teach Your Children' before moving The Grateful Dead towards country. When they reverted to psychedelic type, he indulged his country leanings with side project The New Riders Of The Purple Sage.

History shows that The Eagles were far and away the most successful practitioners of country-rock. By applying lush harmonies and a commercial sheen to their songs, plus the benefit of shrewd management and a thrusting label boss in David Geffen, they broke sales records through the Seventies and inspired a host of soundalikes. As Poco guitarist Paul Cotton explained to author John Einarson in the book *Desperados: The Roots Of Country Rock*, "The Eagles had that pop door open, and we wanted to rock on in . . . we knew there was only so much you could do with country and it was bound to happen, especially after seven or eight albums."

Gram Parsons' harmony singer Emmylou Harris retained her major-label recording contract through the Eighties, a difficult decade for country-rock. Video-led releases were now the norm, and pop's concentration on image flew in the face of country-rock's emotion and sincerity. Steve Earle won a foothold by crossing over to rock into a position Bruce Springsteen had held a decade or so earlier, but the likes of The Long Ryders, Jason & The Scorchers and The Beat Farmers found it tougher going. It would take rough and ready indie groups like The Replacements to find a middle ground between rock and roots music, while The Blasters,

Rank And File and The Knitters (the country alter-ego of LA new wavers X) also showed promise.

The Indigo Girls' Amy Ray believes that the alignment between alt.country and punk in the States is "because of recording style, more than aesthetics and songwriting; The Replacements were sort of alt.country in their own right." Her 2001 solo album *Stag* owed something to the genre, which she attributes to the fact that, "I had to record it fast and I think that's what gives it that Whiskeytown, acoustic feel."

She may just be onto something. Illinois band Uncle Tupelo recorded their best album, *March 16–20, 1992*, in the space of that five-day period. Their music merged punk and country, "but not intentionally – that's just what came out." They emerged from indie rock to tour incessantly and make four records. The first – 1990's *No Depression*, named after a Thirties Carter Family hillbilly song – would, five years later, inspire a magazine which found its title used generically to describe a musical movement. With no little irony, the mag's first issue coincided with the demise of Uncle Tupelo, who broke up on the cusp of commercial success: songwriters Jeff Tweedy and Jay Farrar started their own bands, respectively Wilco and Son Volt, and it was an early shot of the latter that would grace the cover.

The growth of what became known in the Nineties as alt.country was accelerated in Chicago, traditional home of the blues. That's where three people scraped and saved to release a 17-track sampler featuring local bands and artists of a vaguely country-ish persuasion. Subtitled A Compilation of Chicago Insurgent Country Bands, *For A Life Of Sin* was the first release of the nascent Bloodshot records label.

Its release alerted a plethora of unsigned US acts to the fact that there was a home for them to go to, and the likes of The Mekons, Neko Case and Kelly Hogan soon found their way into the company's release schedule. As always happens, however, major labels started taking an interest and acts like The Old 97s and Robbie Fulks signed elsewhere for bigger bucks. The experience wasn't entirely agreeable for the latter, who returned in time to pen an ode to his once and future label's fifth birthday: 'Bloodshot's Turning

Five': 'They took the twang of a steel guitar/A little trendy left-wing jive/And they made a sound that the whole world loves/ Now Bloodshot's turning five.' In Fulks' words, Bloodshot "figured out a niche, and stuck to it."

Founder Rob Miller believed Bloodshot's main contribution was the fact that "these days there's more acceptance of the notion that country music isn't appalling. Roots music has always had an ebb and flow, but I think it's become less of a curiosity now."

The website Americana-UK.com (which is well worth investigation) gave up compiling their Top 10 artists of the year list for 2001 since only ten of their respondents voted for anyone other than Ryan Adams. This left the other 90-something per cent registering the name of the former Whiskeytown singer, usually followed by 'Who else?' in brackets. Most generic websites would cool on an artist who had so obviously made the break to the mainstream, but not Americana-UK.com:

"Ryan's transition from small-time to big is one of those great phenomena – nobody knows quite how it happened or why (let's face it, if it was because of great songs, then a million other people like Witness and The Pernice Brothers would be number one for weeks). But it has, and as a pioneer for a genre he's still just about associated with, he's perfect."

And breaking into the mainstream remained the major conundrum for *No Depression*/alt.country outfits. The movement had seemed to reach something of a peak in 1996. A debate at that year's SXSW festival titled 'Alt.country: The State of Twang' concluded that the genre's most successful albums achieved sales figures of less than 50,000 copies – more than modest compared to sales in other major genres. "If we're a success," one debater concluded, "then we're going to go broke."

Other members of the panel pointed out that the Soundscan in-store sales registration system downgraded sales at independent stores and at concerts as opposed to chains. But though a Dallas radio station had recently become the nation's first full-time 'Americana' station, there was no real prospect of the music gaining the airplay to get over to the hitherto unconverted. With these problems to surmount, the genre developed what some would describe as a do-it-yourself attitude and others as a ghetto mentality.

It was this that Ryan Adams would have to surmount in his attempt to find fame and fortune. The likes of Hazeldine and Calexico had failed to break through and, though The Jayhawks had won a major-label contract, creative differences between their two singer-songwriters (commerciality versus authenticity) scuppered their progress at a vital stage. Ryan's emergence from his band Whiskeytown to become a fully fledged solo star filled the gap admirably.

Broadcaster Bob Harris has done much to educate Britain in the joys of alt.country, and sees Adams' career as echoing his own involvement with the genre. "My absolute plug-in moment happened when we started *Bob Harris Country* on Radio 2 in April 1999, and Ryan is the perfect artist to play because he's operating on the fringes of country," he says. "The alt.country movement is a growing energy, no doubt about that, and his emergence has given them a focus. So Ryan's been quite an important figurehead for me in terms of my own thinking."

Harris hosts a more mainstream show on Saturday nights and has found listeners "moving across from Saturday to Thursday and saying, 'If this is country music I actually quite *like* it!' It's not the big hat, Nashville factory-produced stuff, but it owes a nod to the heritage of country. Ryan is very aware of the tradition of the music and you can tell that in the instrumental make-up and feel of the songs – there's no doubt about that."

The DJ believes bringing people to the fringes of country from the mainstream is a very important factor in the continuing growth of the music. "I have never seen any genre as being an enclave, and I feel a particular pleasure and energy that people are coming to my country show on Thursday nights from rock or other areas to discover there's much about Ryan Adams' type of country music that they can feel and identify with. Ryan's doing such a great job – unwittingly of course, he's just following his own individual course – but for me he assumes more significance than that."

Harris illustrates his point with a definitive example of the 'Adams Effect'. "When I was promoting my autobiography last year I had a guy called Brian, about my age, who was my driver for a couple of nights. We were talking in the car and he was saying, like so many of my contemporaries who maybe don't listen to my shows, that there's no good music around nowadays, it all expired in the Seventies . . . that was the golden age and music nowadays is absolute rubbish. We were going to Borders and I said, 'When we get to Borders go off and buy yourself the new album by Ryan Adams.' Like everybody else, he went, 'Bryan Adams?' No, *Ryan* Adams! It's an album called *Gold*. If this doesn't single-handedly restore your faith in present-day music I don't know what will.

"So at the end of my talk he appeared at the back of the crowd holding this album up with a smile on his face. He'd bought it. We got in the car and I made him wait until we got on the motorway to play it. I didn't even let him set it up with 'New York, New York' . . . 'Rosalie Come And Go' was the track I wanted him to hear first. We got onto the slip road and I said, 'Right, Brian, press that button!' And we drove along in silence; obviously the track was playing but we weren't discussing it at all. As it finished, I caught his eye in the rear-view mirror and said, 'C'mon Brian, what do you think?' He looked at me and said, 'Faaan-*tastic*', just like that.

"So it had jumped the generation gap, jumped the country culture gap, to a guy who was convinced there was nothing particularly creative going on. He played the whole album as we drove home and said, 'You're right, this *has* restored my faith. I'm gonna get everything this guy has done. He's absolutely brilliant.' There we are. My 19-year-old son likes him too – he's fantastic."

If Ryan Adams has more in common with the 'Outlaws' of country – Willie Nelson and Waylon Jennings, two of the personalities who, in the Seventies, promoted the claims of Austin as a country-music centre to rival Nashville – then that's no surprise. Because they, too, vaulted the barrier between country and the musical mainstream when *Wanted! The Outlaws*, a 1976 release with Jesse Colter and Tompall Glaser, became the first country album to sell a million.

Ryan Adams may well be the first country outlaw to have made it big in the current millennium, and it's no surprise that a new country-related magazine, *Mavericks*, put him on their cover as

2002 closed. It might not be as significant a crowning as Uncle Tupelo on *No Depression* some seven or eight years earlier, but it proved that the movement had legs – even if its biggest and brightest stars would eventually escape its universe.

2

Jacksonville Skyline

SUITABLY FOR A man who's been creating musical fireworks out of the box, David Ryan Adams took his first breath on Bonfire Night, November 5, 1974, in Jacksonville, North Carolina. Ironically, his near-namesake Bryan was also born that day in Kingston, Ontario, albeit 15 years earlier – but equally coincidentally, and certainly of more musical relevance, it was one year to the day since a 27-year-old Gram Parsons breathed his last.

His home town of some 30,000 inhabitants on the North Carolina coastal plains is one of which Adams has dismissively said "most of the people think that at night the sun goes around the moon". The presence of a US Marine base, with its rapidly rotating personnel, hardly added to the attraction. He came up with an evocative soundbite while talking to the late Timothy White of *Billboard* magazine in early 2001, just after the release of his first solo album *Heartbreaker*.

"It would hit night-time, and there's just absolutely nothing there. It's bleak and can be extraordinarily beautiful, but it's very remote and slow. There's lots of pine trees, and it's flat because it's below sea level, and it can make you crazy with this total sense of calm outside . . . but at the same time this sense of urgency, like you're just lost in the whole world. I think it turns a lot of people there to drink. There have been times when I've actually needed to go back to that feeling of calm there. Then it'd wear off real fast, and I'd run like hell."

It's clearly been a rather more complex relationship than that. In other interviews, he appears to have reconciled himself to the place, even crediting it with lyrical inspiration in a revealing 'autobiographical fragment' posted on an Internet bulletin board long before Timothy White took an interest. "Most all of the songs I write now concern Jacksonville. For a very long time I wouldn't write about it or even think about it because I had a very hard time growing up there. And the town itself has been going through a very hard time since before I was born. But I dropped out of high school there, I bought my first records there and I will probably die and be buried there eventually.

"For some reason I can identify with that place now – all those fucking people live there because they can't imagine living anyplace else. It's all they know and they're scared and don't like change. So that place is inhabited by all these old-fashioned people with ideas about the world that just aren't viable anyplace else. They all drink a lot or not. It is the oldest, wrongest place in the world, it's where I'm from and it's where my songs are coming from."

Adams has characterised himself on several occasions as "a shark . . . I have to move forward or die". And while his musical career has seen some wild stylistic swings to back up that assertion, it's the reconciliation of his need to break new ground and his respect and fascination for tradition, as exemplified by the area in which he grew up, that has provided some interesting moments.

The major figure in his early life was his mother, Susan, who was left to raise three children when his father, building contractor Robert Adams, left home. (Ryan was then nine.) Many years later, Ryan nominated her as his hero in a *Mojo* magazine survey in preference to any formative musical influence. Her major attributes, he explained, were leaving books around the house for him to read while he was growing up, and the fact that she was "a complete realist, but not afraid to be a dreamer" – traits he contends she passed on to him.

Other heroes he met through the books his English-teacher mother intended him to discover included the Beat Poet strain of Jack Kerouac, Allen Ginsberg and Ken Kesey. On a slightly different literary tack, he devoured the works of Edgar Allan Poe, Emily Dickinson and Sylvia Plath (who would turn up in a song on the *Gold* album some two decades later). It was all grist to the youngster's mill, Southern playwrights Eudora Welty and Tennessee Williams becoming particular favourites. Then there was Henry Miller, whose books he read "not because of his perversions but his lust for life." His childhood roll of honour was completed by his art teacher, "a great painter", and friends "who could skateboard really well." Creativity was the key for a boy who was "getting into art about as heavily as my friends were getting into chicks."

He enjoyed "a perfectly Southern upbringing, like Norman Rockwell crossed with *Steel Magnolias* and crickets chirping everywhere." Yet under the surface of Jacksonville life lurked a more sinister undercurrent – and, having read his mum's textbook on abnormal psychology by the age of 10, Ryan was well prepared to transcend it. "My first crush was a black girl and, when they saw us holding hands, they removed her from my class! It was all masked by this veiled racism. That stuff always broke my heart, man. I had to get out of there, out of my hometown. People are acting out this *Planet Of The Apes* shit, stuff that was going on in the fucking Sixties. I was like, this is grotesque, how uneducated."

An important musical epiphany occurred at age 13, when one of his skateboarder chums was left a crateful of albums by a relation. Offered a rummage once his pal had taken his pick, he lighted on The Smiths' compilation album *Hatful Of Hollow*. With art a big thing in his life, it's not so surprising the cover was what drew Ryan in – but what he found on the vinyl between the square-foot of card was beyond price. "I couldn't believe the lyrics," he recalled, still wide-eyed years later.

Next stop was *Meat Is Murder*, the band's 1985 offering, which was even more to his liking. Having played it first in his mother's car tape player en route from Wilmington to Jacksonville, it would remain a favourite thereafter. "It's a completely perfect work and it's got such humour," he'd confide to *Uncut*'s Nigel Williamson as part of that magazine's Pet Sounds feature in late 2001. Significantly, the track he most related to was 'The Headmaster Ritual', "about wanting to break out of the parameters of school – and I must have played 'That Joke Isn't Funny Anymore' a million times."

Interestingly for a group member who, like Morrissey, had found his first serious outfit too small to hold him, he praised this as "a proper group record . . . they had an amazing chemistry. I consider myself a sketch artist compared to the Smiths." The band left such a mark that the very first track of his first solo album, *Heartbreaker,* is entitled 'An Argument With David Rawlings Concerning Morrissey' . . . and is just that!

Ryan's first instrument – drums, which he took up at the age of 14 – was his entry ticket to a band, Blank Label, but the combination failed to satisfy his creative stirrings. A three-track seven-inch disc has since emerged, dated 1991, featuring Shane Duhe (vocals, guitar), Michelle Horn (bass) and Jere McIlwean (guitar, of whom more anon), with Ryan on drums. The tracks, recorded at Fastrack Studios in Verona, North Carolina, are titled 'Non-Existence', 'Sonic Issue' and 'JLW', but it's not known if any of these were Adams compositions.

A skateboard trade with a friend's brother the following year ("I probably still owe him a hundred and fifty bucks") brought a "terrible" Les Paul copy called a Memphis into his possession, and his first songwriting efforts followed as surely as night succeeds day. "It made me feel cool to play guitar and write songs," he'd later reflect, adding that "if you couldn't get hold of drugs or sex you had to do *something.*" Not, he'd later reflect, that Jacksonville was a hotbed of musical activity: "When I grew up, you were lucky to find a copy of *Rolling Stone* in town."

The catalyst for the move to music from skateboarding had been going to see Pumphouse, Jacksonville's only punk group at that time. Besides, "You can't skateboard every day because it rains, so you start a band. And then you can't skateboard every day because you've got band practice . . ."

The influences at work on the young Ryan Adams were nothing if not disparate. His grandmother, in her innocence, had bought him his first vinyl, an (unspecified) Black Sabbath album of all things. The first he'd been inspired to buy himself was The Dead Kennedys' *In God We Trust,* followed by discs by Corrosion Of Conformity and Sonic Youth. These, of course, were in addition to *Hatful Of Hollow.* He also started buying punk albums from local pawn shops to augment his collection, picking up on a musical trend many were already putting down.

In the frequent, unavoidable absence of his mother, Ryan's grandmother (or 'Geemaw', in local parlance) Dedmond was a readily available sounding board when it came to music. "We talked about a lot of stuff when I was young," he'd later confirm. "She'd play me Willie Nelson records, and I would play her Black Flag records, and she'd say, 'They love to hit those cymbals, don't they?' It was really cool, and my rapport with her was that we just sort of were open with everything." (Adams' love for Black Flag lives on in one of two tattoos on his left arm, the other of fellow LA punks X, while he would duet with Willie Nelson on a 2002 TV special.)

Adams had been writing prose and poetry from the age of eight, using his grandmother's old typewriter. "I started writing short stories when I was really into Edgar Allan Poe. Then later, when I was a teenager, I got really hard into cult fiction: Hubert Selby Jr, Henry Miller, Jack Kerouac. There wasn't," he explained, "much else to do in Jacksonville. There was skateboarding. Vandalism. Then you go inner. At least *I* did."

He would spend an increasing amount of time at Geemaw Dedmond's after his parents split up, loving her "smoke-filled house with old hi-fi's and lamps with dust on them." They would stay up late, watch re-runs of George Burns and Woody Allen TV shows, play card games and discuss philosophy. His relationship with his mother was the typical up-and-down stuff of teenagehood: he'd later recall the time she "called the cops on me for being wasted when I was 16", while much time was spent "behind the Dairy Queen (store) down the street from my house: I used to drink (there) when everyone else was asleep." A typical childhood, then . . .

In high school, he was excluded from class for wearing a T-shirt with a melting ice cube and the slogan 'Christianity is stupid . . . give up'. That teacher's reaction was far from isolated, and he dropped out in the first week of his tenth grade, moving soon after into a friend's grandmother's old plantation house, just outside of town. While in this 'punk-rock commune', he continued to read, listen to records and skateboard.

Country music found its way into the teenage Ryan Adams' life "like facial hair. Just woke up one day and there it was." His grandmother certainly favoured the music, at least on the odd occasion she could beat the punk of the family to the record player. He felt the same connection with country veteran Loretta Lynn (of *Coalminers Daughter* bio-pic fame) as he did with his punk heroes. "Listening to her, I get the same feeling as when I'm listening to Bad Brains. It's the same pathos."

But before his own move to the country camp occurred there would be short spells in two local bands, Ass and The Lazy Stars. The latter was an outfit he's likened in interviews to "Spacemen 3 and The Replacements – at the same time", bassist Tom Cushman and drummer John Douglas making up the numbers. In the autumn of 2001, an 11-track CD of music supposedly made by this line-up in 1994 was advertised on Internet auction site ebay with the following announcement:

"Before Whiskeytown, and somewhere between one of the Patty Duke Syndrome's break up/make ups, there was Lazy Stars. Bassist Tom Cushman recorded them on a tape he stole from a car, and it has magically been transferred to digital. Anguished post-punk power drone rock, like Crazy Horse, Wipers, Galaxie 500. 11 Songs. Rare, raw, nice. Yes, this is Ryan on all vocals and guitar."

The tracks, released under the (probably retrospective) title *Exile On Daisy Street*, included two versions apiece of 'Brand New Shoes', 'Blue Door' and 'Withering Heights', while other titles were 'Pack Of Smokes', 'Old Stereo', 'The Birds', 'Hill' and 'Burnt Bed'. At the time of writing, they had not made it to the wider world.

Next for Ryan Adams lay a two-year stint with Patty Duke. His partner in crime was one Jere (pronounced Jerry) McIlwean. As Ryan later explained to *No Depression* editor Peter Blackstock, the pair were nothing less than small-town kindred spirits. "I was growing up a freak, this weird music person, and in that town, there was no one like me. Except Jere."

McIlwean, already 20-something to Adams' 16, was bass player with previously mentioned punk band Pumphouse. By day, he worked at the Record Bar store, where Ryan was one of his best customers with a diverse shopping list of Half Japanese and Sonic Youth albums. Eventually curiosity got the better of the older lad, as Adams recalls. "One day he just asked me, 'Why in the hell are you buying these records?' I said, 'Because I *like* 'em.'

"We hit it off, and next thing I knew he took me out to his place where he had all this musical equipment, and we started that band. Our drummer, Alan Midgett, had this big old barn where we played music at all hours of the night." Adams and McIlwean apparently wrote four songs together at their very first attempt at collaboration, sealing their creative union.

The Patty Duke Syndrome's progress on the Jacksonville bar scene was halted when Adams acquired the necessary qualifications to leave school (which had taken a poor second place to his musical activities to date) and move to the state capital of Raleigh (pronounced Ray-leigh), an hour and a half's drive south-east of his home town. Its well-to-do neighbour Chapel Hill was a mere ten to fifteen minutes away and the combination of Raleigh, Chapel Hill and Jacksonville boasted a thriving indie music scene.

Known as 'The Triangle', the three towns had attracted press attention in the aftermath of Seattle's grunge boom as the likely next birthplace of a musical trend. Not that such national notoriety seemed to affect the atmosphere of an area that had already spawned bands like lo-fi heroes Superchunk, noisy indie-rockers The Archers Of Loaf and neo-rockabillies Southern Culture On The Skids and Flat Duo Jets.

Long before that, in the Sixties, customers at a Chapel Hill venue known as the Cat's Cradle Coffee House had been serenaded by The Fabulous Corsairs, alias singer-songwriter brothers James and Alex Taylor (whose father was Dean of the University's medical school), while Don Dixon, later to become known as R.E.M.'s first producer, served his musical apprenticeship in the ranks of local legends Arrogance. The following decade had brought the talents of two other musician-producers, Mitch Easter and Chris Stamey, to national attention. Both fronted bands, The dB's and Let's Active respectively, before becoming backroom boys in the industry. The name of Stamey, in particular, would crop up several times in the Ryan Adams story.

The opportunities the Triangle offered a budding musician struck Adams as "*amazing*: there must have been 30 bands in between the cities. Any night you could see a band, either playing at the Fallout Shelter or the Brewery." Certainly, the area had earned a reputation that made it, in the words of *The Rough Guide to Music USA*, "a place where creative minds could germinate the seeds of something groundbreaking and unique." This was underlined by the breakthrough in early 1997 of The Ben Folds Five, a Chapel Hill three-piece whose stance was as unconventional as their deliberately misleading name and whose second album *Whatever And Ever Amen* became a worldwide best-seller.

A crucial fact that made Raleigh more conducive to musical activity than small-town Jacksonville was the presence of the North Carolina State University. The cheap accommodation favoured by the cash-strapped students tended to be off the main drag, known as Hillsborough Street, and one such thoroughfare was to be the inspiration for Ryan's first set of recorded songs, Whiskeytown's *Faithless Street*. It was a wonderful new world.

For his few months in this new environment, he'd be confined to sleeping on friends' sofas, living for weeks on a diet of potato soup and alcohol. When not working as a restaurant dishwasher or digging ditches for a plumbing company to keep body and soul together, he participated in a couple of bands he later described as being "along the lines of The Replacements and The Minutemen".

Adams' reputation for being a workaholic stems from around this time when, as he now recalls, he'd been playing in two or three different local outfits at once. "I'd have a band that'd be on tour and they'd have one that would play every other month," he'd remark, suggesting being a working musician was making him unpopular on the scene. But he seemed to thrive on being someone who had "a life that is music, not a life with music as a hobby."

Names of the small-time groups he graced in this period include American Rock Highway and Cotton TV Land. But these outfits (which were destined to remain just names) clearly had little potential and, when bassist McIlwean followed his lead and moved to Raleigh, Patty Duke was swiftly re-formed.

Brian Walsby, a refugee from the West Coast punk scene,

replaced Alan Midgett on drums, though the Jacksonville sticksman remained on friendly terms and would later provide Adams with pre-production assistance on solo début *Heartbreaker*. Playing with Walsby provided a temporary cachet, since his previous bands included Wwax (*sic*), containing future Superchunk singer/guitarist Ralph 'Mac' McCaughan, and indie favourites Willard.

Interviewed by *Magnet* magazine years later, Walsby recalled his first impressions of Ryan Adams – and they were far from favourable. "He was a hyperactive, spazzy, smelly little kid who I thought was full of shit. Someone who just *couldn't* be as enthusiastic as he appeared." One night at Chapel Hill club the Cat's Cradle, where nationally known acts often played with local support, the drummer had his conversation with Mac McCaughan interrupted by a rampant Ryan, who wanted an old single by Wwax autographed. Most heinous of all crimes, however, was the fact that, "He talked with him like he'd known him forever." (Interestingly, McCaughan had formed his own indie label, Merge Records, with bassist bandmate Laura Ballance in 1989, so maybe he saw an opportunity.)

Raleigh proved a fertile stamping ground for the Patty Duke Syndrome, though they broke up four times during an 18-month period. "We didn't like each other at all," Ryan would recall, likening the mix of personalities to "piss in vinegar. But we were the shit in Raleigh for a while. And I was just 18. I couldn't believe it." Fights between the band members tended to be over girls rather than musical disagreements but, since they were selling out clubs and a record deal was in the wind, a little personal animosity was a small price for local heroes to pay. (An Adams song about the period, titled 'Bastards I Used To Know', remains unrecorded.)

There also seemed to be friction between the two frontmen regarding Adams' fondness for a drink: bear in mind here that the legal age for alcohol consumption is 21 in the States, unlike 18 in Britain. Drummer Walsby (who would go on to play with the band Polvo) sided with McIlwean, thinking Adams an "over-boisterous drunk", but McIlwean's righteous indignation hid a more serious problem. "If I had one beer," Ryan recalled, "Jere would get mad as hell at me. And then I come to find the whole time he's a closet heroin addict. And he ended up dying."

The break-up of the Patty Duke Syndrome in 1994 had been pretty inevitable. "We weren't getting along any more. I just had a lot of intense things in my personal life that sort of took their toll." Their sole recorded legacy was a seven-inch single, 'Texas'/ 'History', split with Glamourpuss on the Blast-O-Platter label and released in 1994. If you haven't heard it (and most of us haven't), "It really was just like the rock stuff in Whiskeytown, but a little faster. I was a punk-ass kid, for sure, but I wasn't a proper punk. I didn't have a mohawk or anything. It really was more like post-punk, I'd say . . . almost just really loud pop."

Ryan recalls writing his first song for Patty Duke when he was 16, describing them as an "arty noise punk band . . . when I started to get more into songwriting it got into more of a Hüsker Dü-influenced band. We got a lot of comparisons to them which I didn't mind." The combined processes of becoming old enough to drink and going through relationships changed his world view and, consequently, the nature of his musical output. "I went through this really, really bad period of my life where I was really sad and it's really hard to play that kind of music, you know, or to have all that energy when it's drained from you because you are having such a bad time . . . Country music is really healing for that kind of stuff. That's just kind of like what I started writing as a sort of reflection. I didn't plan on doing it."

He'd later reflect that country was part of his surroundings. "That kind of music hangs like a blanket over Jacksonville and I'd like to secretly have more in common with that town and those people . . ." His choice of recreational listening – Loretta Lynn, George Jones, Lefty Frizzell, Roy Acuff, Johnny Cash and Merle Haggard – had already begun to cross over to his own music. "I really wanted pedal steel on a couple of our tracks on our tape but we just couldn't find anybody to play it."

Adams wrote the song 'Theme For A Trucker' about McIlwean, who joined a retro-punk band called Trucker after the Patty Duke Syndrome broke up. This was performed by Whiskeytown on a soundtrack called *The End Of Violence*, released by Bloodshot Records, as well as appearing on a short EP under the same name. (A slow, acoustic song with Caitlin Cary prominent on fiddle, this song has been played only a couple of times post-Whiskeytown by Ryan at solo shows in 1999 and 2000.)

Adams remained a fan, if not a close friend, of McIlwean. "(Trucker) were like an MC5 and Bad Brains-influenced band. Hearing them would give you chills; you could feel something was gonna happen, like they were gonna change the world. And damned if he didn't go and die on everybody. I wanted to write about it for a long time, and then finally I started writing that song. He'd hate that song so bad; he *hated* country. Well, he didn't hate country music, but he didn't like my version of it, anyway."

A local North Carolina entertainment website summed up the PDS thus: "The members came from utterly different circumstances – Brian Walsby from the hectic West Coast punk scene, Ryan Adams and Jere McIlwean from the rural splendour of downstate NC – and the resulting music documented the tension between those two worlds in every note. During their short existence they broke up at least a half-dozen times, but while they were together, they recorded some of the tightest post-punk around. Thanks to both the interpersonal tension and the music, it's easy and tempting to raise the spectre of Hüsker Dü – but the songs never dive into the depths of anguish that Bob Mould always seemed to be in."

Parallel with Ryan's punk predilections ran a love of classic rock, and he recalls rediscovering The Rolling Stones as a key moment of this period. It was thanks to Lazy Stars' bassist, Tom Cushman, "who was a huge fan". Having stopped listening to the band while under the influence of art-rock and Sonic Youth, he stumbled on *Exile On Main Street* one snowy winter's day. The song that made the impression was 'I Just Want To See His Face' and, after playing it 20 times (doubtless to the bemusement of his neighbours) he'd reconnected to the wellspring of rock'n'roll. "I'll never be able to detach myself from that song . . . it makes me want time to stand still."

As far as image went, Ryan similarly took his cues from the late Sixties/early Seventies. "There's a consensus in rock'n'roll that Keith Richards, Patti Smith and The Velvet Underground looked cool," he'd remark, adding them to Sonic Youth in his list of style role models.

All had been going well – maybe *too* well – for the teenager, who admits to having been "pretty cocky, but I had every reason to be." He had his own place at $200 a month ("people smoked crack downstairs, but I kept my door locked"), plus a good looking girlfriend ("Melanie . . . she had red hair for *days*"). But all good things come to an end, and the relationship foundered at just about the same time as the band. At least this double blow could be used as inspiration for songs. "Somehow," he says, "I started listening to the kind of music I'd heard growing up: the Stanley Brothers, Hank Williams, Willie Nelson. And then I started playing my version of that kind of music."

The name Space Madness should be mentioned before we go much further, as an 11-song tape, *The Space Madness Demos*, showed up in trading circles in April 2002. The material on it was believed to be recorded in 1994. The music was definitely pre-Whiskeytown and featured Ryan (or, if not, certainly a soundalike) singing on most, if not all of the tracks. The other personnel listed were Thompson King and Tristan Andreas, presumably on bass and drums, though the jury is out as to whether the band was called Space Madness or The Skylarks.

Song titles were as follows: 'Lost Highway', 'If I Had A Reason', 'Snowflakes Dancing', 'Lonesomeville', 'Fifth Of Liquor', 'Zebra Room', 'Found A Job Today', 'Hazel Country Scarecrow', 'Gold Stratocaster', 'Industry Town' and 'Poor Southern Girl'. 'Lost Highway', of course, predicts his current record label, while 'Lonesomeville' could be some relation to Whiskeytown . . . but that's supposition.

Certainly, the title 'Found A Job Today' had some relevance. Past part-time posts Ryan had tried included working in restaurants, repairing furniture and house painting, as well as working as an office boy for the *Raleigh News & Observer*. These jobs were "the kind that I expected to either quit or be fired from. They served the purpose of playing bills at that time and my interest in the job began and ended there. For some reason I am one of those people who cannot be satisfied giving into routine. I get restless."

On the demise of Patty Duke, and with a rent cheque to find, Ryan found work in a bakery, starting at four each morning and putting loaves on racks for a nine-hour shift at eight dollars fifty an hour. Understandably, he very soon lost touch with everyone on the music scene, having to hit the sack no later than eight each evening. But initially, at least, he revelled in it, or at least the regular wage it delivered, taking care of such mundane business as having his front teeth, which had been broken in a long-ago childhood accident, properly capped. Maybe, after all, his recklessness had subsided.

But when the bakery, impressed by his work, started prodding him up the management ladder, he came to his senses about a job that was "monotonous as fuck and as American as you can get." It was time to get back on the rock'n'roll bandwagon. A pal in Boise, Idaho, called him and invited him to fill the guitar-playing vacancy in his band but, while weighing up the option, he found something to his liking closer to home.

The next stop on the twisted road to fame and fortune would be Whiskeytown.

3

A Heady Brew

"All the members of Whiskey Town (sic) have done time on that weird line between the Old and New South, the point where rural blends to urban, where the strip-malls sit cheek-by-jowl with the feed-and-seed. It inspires the angriest kind of punk-rock frustration, but tempered with a genuine, if perverse, love for all the decaying trappings of tradition.

"The result is country music with a fixation on ennui, or punk rock with an unhealthy respect for the past. Put concretely: their good-natured honky-tonk cover of Black Flag's 'Nervous Breakdown' is every bit as good as the original – and a lot safer to dance to."

(From the website of North Carolina Multimedia Exhibition of Musicians and Entertainers)

WHISKEYTOWN GREW FROM a chance discussion in a Raleigh sandwich shop cum bar called Sadlacks much favoured by University students and, in Ryan's words, "a complete crazy, obnoxiously strange place where everyone hangs out". It was the kind of informal joint whose garden in the summer would be inhabited by at least a couple of long-hairs and their guitars picking out a tune. Not that Ryan Adams, who'd be out of town in a matter of days, looked like being one . . . until fate took a hand.

Emporium owner Eric Gilmore, who acquired the affectionate nickname of Skillet due to his finely honed culinary skills, had heard Ryan was up for starting a country-punk band, and, leaning over the counter, offered his services. "The band started with me and Skillet and this guy named Rags playing banjo," Adams told *No Depression* magazine. "And then, his room-mate, Brian, became the bass player, and we were a 'coffee-country band'. That's what Skillet called it.

"It was a three-piece electric band; it sounded kinda like The

Gun Club, a little bit like Uncle Tupelo. We called it coffee-country because we were really wired. We'd get a 12-pack (of beer) and drink about three cups of coffee, and get stoned and get drunk. And by the time all the chemicals got in us, we were playing pretty fast."

The Miller Hi Life beer the bar owner bought Adams to seal the deal would, in a small but significant way, change the course of musical history. As for influences, Gilmore was feeding Adams' musical muse as well as his body, playing him Gram Parsons every time he called in "for (pre-noon) early beers". A framed 12-inch album cover of Parsons' *Grievous Angel* would soon adorn the wall of Adams' apartment alongside one by Fleetwood Mac, neatly encapsulating his ongoing musical duality.

"I think I had more of an American Music Club idea in my head when we started Whiskeytown," he recalls, "although everyone else's ideas definitely changed it to be more country. I wanted to use pedal steel, fiddles and accordion and whatever we could get our hands on, just to make a really cool mood for all the songs that I was going to write."

As for the evocative name of Whiskeytown, Adams – as ever – had a story. "Down here, when somebody gets really fucked up, they put the word 'town' on the end of something – like, 'God-damn, that guy's fuckin' coketown' or something. Or you'd go like, 'God, I was so stoned, man, it was like fuckin' hallucinationtown.' And you'd go, 'God, man, we had so much liquor that night, we were fuckin' whiskeytown.' My girlfriend of the time hated it, and I thought that was a great reason to keep the name."

Alcohol would play a major role in fuelling Whiskeytown stage performances. They would, by Adams' own admission, often show up at their gigs the worse for drink "because we thought it was funny, not because we had to have a beer. I was like, 'This is ridiculous. You're *paying* me to do this? Fuck that. I'm gonna get *so* drunk . . .' Everybody did. We didn't care at all. So by the time that we ended up maybe caring, it didn't even matter any more."

Whiskeytown, then, stood for drunk, loaded, fucked up – take your pick, as well as "a fictional place where everybody was drunk." So, instead of heading to Boise, Ryan Adams found himself holding down a job in a very real place, Sadlacks, while dreaming of a glorious musical future in the mythical Whiskeytown.

At their best, Whiskeytown mixed punk intensity with the unashamed emotion of country music, which came from listening to the MC5 as much as listening to George Jones. Adams' one-word description of the result was "unpredictable . . . we don't have a sound. We can't even figure out how to work our amplifiers half the time . . . We just play and see what happens." Near enough was good enough, it seems. "This band is probably more punk than my old (Patty Duke) band because my old band used to be in tune."

Back in those formative months, the catalyst for Whiskeytown to leave the drawing board was the arrival of Phil Wandscher, whose talents encompassed guitar, harmonica and vocals. He was another Skillet Gilmore room-mate, but his musical leanings were very much more rock-oriented than bassist Brian or, indeed, the banjo-playing Rags, both of whom would fade from the scene.

Wandscher had no band experience to draw from, a six-year stint with the North Carolina Boys Choir the one and only item of substance on his musical CV. Perhaps because of this, he tended to be a straight talker. Majorly influenced by The Rolling Stones, the older boy obviously felt he was to be the senior partner.

And right from the outset, the relationship between Adams and Wandscher was to be a fraught one. The way Adams remembers it, they were both drunk in a bar one night and Wandscher declared he was "gonna play guitar in your band". A bought beer, as ever, clinched the deal. "But I always hated Phil . . . I thought he was a fuckin' jerk." For his part, Wandscher recalled the Adams he met in a band biography as "a 16-, 17-year-old brat . . . he's *still* a brat."

Steve Grothman, a bass-playing friend of Wandscher, was next to join, tilting the balance of power further away from Adams, while Caitlin Cary, whose fiddle and vocals gave them a decidedly country element – an Emmylou Harris to Adams' Gram Parsons – was a University student studying Creative Writing who was addicted to bluegrass.

Her addition to the Whiskeytown ranks was down to Adams, who was alerted to her talents by a mutual friend named Hal Hammond. "I had just moved to Raleigh and was definitely not an insider," she told *Magnet* magazine in 2001. What was more, she'd never played in a band before with the exception of The Garden Weasels, a college outfit she describes as a "jokey country covers band".

Music had, however, been an important part of her life since a childhood spent in Seville, Ohio with six older brothers. One, Peter, took her under his musical wing early on and encouraged her to learn the violin. The music played around the house was predominantly Irish, and this was soon to come through in her playing. "I've had people say that my style isn't really country, that the lines are longer and more melodic," she said on an early Whiskeytown press release. "That's the Irish influence."

After graduating, she'd spent a year in Richmond, Virginia, where she made her solo singing début performing Tom Petty's 'Refugee' at a benefit for Gulf War victims. But fiction writing was her aim when she enrolled at North Carolina State – little realising she was about to begin a true-life story you just couldn't make up.

"A guy in my English department must have talked to Ryan, because he called me literally out of the blue and told me he was starting a band. He'd heard I played violin and asked would I think about (joining)." Though by her own admission naive, Cary's lack of experience seemed, if anything, to dampen her expectations. "I just thought (being in a band meant) I was gonna have something to do on the weekends. I know the boys in the band probably had a rock'n'roll fantasy, but I never did."

Work and play merged when Caitlin and Ryan (whom she regarded as "a brother in terms of singing and writing . . . a little bratty, *horrible* brother!") were recruited to the ever-changing Sadlacks staff. After their shift was over, they were apt to stay up all night listening to records and planning their future. Not that any of the band members, with the exception of Adams, had aspirations to make a record at this stage. "What we really wanted to do was play, to get paid, to get free booze at the Brewery, the club that pretty much spawned us and got us where we are."

The magic of early Whiskeytown was instantly distilled onto a four-song, 7-inch EP, *Angels*, astonishingly recorded less than two months after they started playing together. This was released in

May of 1995 by local label Mood Food Records, and the title cut, 'Angels Are Messengers From God', would resurface, under the new title of 'Faithless Street', on the album of the same name. The other songs on the EP were 'Tennessee Square', a slow-paced acoustic number in which the singer was 'Drinkin' whiskey in granddaddy's chair . . .', 'Captain Smith' and 'Take Your Guns To Town'.

So impressive were these embryonic first sessions that the whole EP would re-emerge two years later on the *Rural Free Delivery* mini-album, bulked up by a number of further early takes including 'Desperate Ain't Lonely'. The song 'Tennessee Square' would also later reappear in re-recorded form on the *Faithless Street* re-release though this, unlike *Rural Free Delivery*, was undertaken with the band's blessing.

If Whiskeytown on record were good, they could be nothing less than incendiary live. A gig at the Berkeley Cafe in Raleigh in October 1995 ended dramatically with Ryan tossing his vintage Vox guitar into the middle of the room and leaping on it as if it were a skateboard. Then Phil Wandscher jumped from the stage, landing on the still amplified instrument and fatally wounding it in an attack that sounded as bad as it looked. Ryan had meanwhile departed to the cool of an outside patio and so had not seen his axe trashed – but when an onlooker picked it up and brought it to him, instead of freaking out he proceeded to finish the job against the back steps.

As Adams' finances improved he started to build a collection of guitars made in 1974, the year of his birth. He especially treasured a '74 Gibson Firebird, valued at some $4,000, but that too would bite the dust when Whiskeytown ventured north of the border to Vancouver. "It turned into fuckin' matchsticks," he confided to *Guitar* magazine, "in one of those infamous 'Whiskeytown episodes'." But it turned out to be a lesson, albeit an expensive one. "I think I had to do that to realise never to do it again." On the other hand, he reasoned, "I'd rather break a guitar than my hand against a brick wall."

There was certainly an attitude to everything Whiskeytown did, something Ryan explained thus: "People in punk bands around here are starting to do other things because punk rock just gets old after a while." Not old enough, however, to resist the temptation to contribute to a locally produced Richard Hell tribute album, *Who The Hell* (on Cred Factory Records). Their fiddle-laced version of his signature song 'Blank Generation', which also emerged in 1995, began a tradition of many great recordings 'thrown away' and not included on official albums.

Caitlin Cary was rapidly emerging as the counterweight to Ryan's outrageous on-stage behaviour. "I don't think he ever minds that I apologise for him or even make fun of him, which I do. When he does shit like that I go, 'Look at the dumb ass.' And I think he knows that I'm always gonna do that. It doesn't seem to offend him. And it's funny because he's an amazing mind in that anything that he does, he can come up with a very rational sounding argument for why that was the right thing to do. And we'll never actually agree. It's fascinating to listen to him and what goes on in his head. It's endlessly entertaining to me. And I can think of 25 different things in very different areas where we disagree – but then we talk about it and he's got a real good reason why he does the stupid stuff that he does."

Compared with the Patty Duke Syndrome, a three-piece band "into being loud and aggressive", Ryan Adams was now enjoying "learning to arrange songs better", even though the songs themselves "weren't that different". As the band grew and matured, though, he'd find Whiskeytown "turning into almost exactly the same type of band". The crucial difference was that many more people had heard of them.

An accident of fate would mean that, after only having been together six months, they were featured in the first issue of *No Depression*, the 'zine that became the bible of everything alt.country (Fortuitously, market leaders Uncle Tupelo had just decided to split into Son Volt and Wilco). Whiskeytown had been in the right place at the right time to pick up the mantle; indeed, they'd repay the favour by spending March and April of 1997 on the *No Depression* Tour alongside fellow hopefuls The Old '97s, The Picketts and Hazeldine.

And where *No Depression* led, *Rolling Stone* was soon to follow.

In a quote as widely cited as anything about Bruce Springsteen two decades earlier, an impressed critic hailed Whiskeytown as "the Nirvana of alt.country" – or more accurately, "If there's to be a Nirvana among the bands that are impressively dubbed alternative country, look to Whiskeytown." But while he didn't mind being bracketed with Kurt Cobain ("It's flattering, 'cos they were a great band, but I have no intention of blowing my head off"), Ryan detested the alternative country term. "I'm sick to death of that word . . . Country-rock is a better fit, but one that's not altogether accurate either . . ."

The speed at which everything was progressing, from informal coffee-house grouping to a full gig-sheet and national publicity, was something like a fairground ride, and certainly didn't add stability to the enterprise. "Once things kicked in, it went so fast that it was sort of unnatural," said Caitlin at the end of the story. "That's probably at the root of all the Whiskeytown problems. I think Whiskeytown did/does have real magic, but we didn't have time to deal with all our various issues."

The Mood Food label that had brokered their first venture onto vinyl would also be the means by which Whiskeytown's first long-player, *Faithless Street*, came to see the light of day. It was recorded, in Caitlin Cary's words, "in dripping midsummer (of 1995) in a converted barn in Apex, 'the Pinnacle of Good Living', North Carolina." The process took under two weeks from beginning to end at the so-called Funny Farm studio where some strange things undoubtedly happened.

Some of the songs they tackled were already staples of their live set, while others were made up on the spot. For example, Ryan took 20 minutes to scrawl the words of 'Hard Luck Story' on the back of a discarded pizza box and soon afterwards they were cutting the track, vocalising around a single microphone in old-fashioned style. The band's time at the Funny Farm, Cary recalls, went in "kind of a blur: we were all drinking a lot and didn't really know what the hell we were doing."

The entire band shared the songwriting credits on *Faithless Street*, yet Adams would later claim most of the credit for its creation. "Whoever sings the song wrote it," he explained, "so Caitlin wrote

'Matrimony', Phil wrote 'What May Seem Like Love' and 'Top Dollar Blues' (*sic*) and I wrote the rest of the record. The only reason it says 'all songs written by Whiskeytown' is because the guy, Kurt Underhill, from Mood Food Records, didn't know what the hell he was doing."

The songs were, it seems, brought to the band more or less fully formed, though there was co-operation on the finer detail. "Phil would mess around with one part and go, 'I don't know man, let's kind of try this here,' and I'd maybe add some words and then eventually Caitlin might end up adding a word or two or elaborate on an idea." Detailed credits would appear on the album's second incarnation, giving equal weight to Adams solo compositions and collaborations between band members. Only the opening two songs bore Adams and Wandscher's joint names, and then with others.

The whole effort was a band production, with one Greg Woods engineering, though seasoned hand Chris Stamey would take the opportunity to beef up the production values when the album was overhauled for later reissue. Only one guest was featured alongside Adams, Wandscher, Gilmore and Cary – pedal steel guitarist and Nashville session-man Bob Ricker.

In an unusual display of friendship and generosity, Adams would later credit his guitar partner with having produced the record. "At that point, Phil's ear for recording was genuinely amazing. He made our first album be recorded the way *Exile On Main Street* would be recorded. When we went back to find all the original signals, the drums sounded horrible and things like that, but we got all the levels to be good enough to where we actually got to make a good record with it."

The feeling remains that the magic of *Faithless Street*, released in January 1996, came about by happy accident. Caitlin Cary, certainly, rated the results as "serendipitous. As far as the order of the songs (goes), at one point we were drawing (them) out of a hat. We were just going to put them on randomly, but nobody could agree." She, too, credits Phil Wandscher with steering the studio ship to shore. "He was there for the mixing, and he's got a really good ear. He made a lot of executive producer-type decisions that I think were really good."

Ronnie Wood lookalike Greg Woods, the man nominally entrusted with guiding them round the studio, has been labelled by Adams as "a methamphetamine addict and a drunk who didn't quite know what he was but did a great job nonetheless." While the veracity or otherwise of such allegations are open to question, Woods became the subject of some classic rock'n'roll tales, including taking drummer Gilmore for a ride in a light aeroplane and dive-bombing the studio in it "to try to wake us up from our hangovers". Shades of Ozzy Osbourne . . . but fortunately all concerned woke in none the worse shape.

Having fuelled their muse by alcohol – Cary drunk a bottle of whisky one night and rode a horse bareback, but survived the experience intact – Whiskeytown forsook the liquid that gave them their name in favour of the 'upper' drug Benzedrine. "Speed levelled us out and made us better players," claimed Adams, who confesses he's always been amused by the idea that *Faithless Street* "is regarded as such an innocent record" given the excesses that surrounded its creation.

If it was entirely predictable that *Faithless Street* would be acclaimed by *No Depression* as "best début album of the year" – and that in January 1996, its very month of release – the music it contained went a long way to backing up the undoubtedly premature assertion.

If the trick is to save the best till last, then 'Midway Park' had no right being the album's opening cut. Credited (on reissue) to Adams, Wandscher and Gilmore, its picked electric-guitar intro suggests something more stadiumrockish before it's set off by some banjo and Ryan's vocal comes in – almost a Don Henley approach and lighter than the bootlegged demo version which is a rock performance with a capital R.

Continuing in uptempo vein, 'Drank Like A River' gave Caitlin Cary an early chance to shine on upfront harmony vocals. The song's subject, caught "brown bagging it tonight behind some tavern," was drinking himself to an early end after his girl went and married someone else. Again, the emphasis was on rock, thanks to co-writer Phil Wandscher's guitar, Caitlin and Ryan also being credited as writers; the undistinguished ending suggested this was a live favourite they'd taken to the studio.

'Too Drunk To Dream' was laced with Bob Ricker's pedal steel, also allowing the guest musician a retrospective co-songwriting credit with Adams himself. Perhaps significantly, the first song in the running order not to feature Phil Wandscher in the credits stepped tentatively over the line between rock and country. It could well have been a hit if covered by a mainstream country act.

A different voice takes the spotlight with 'What May Seem Like Love', a Wandscher song on which he sings lead with Ryan (by the sound of it) on harmony vocals. It's a passable country strummer with vocals, guitars and pedal steel fighting for supremacy and the occasional dodgy timing – again, very much a live staple performed in the studio exactly as on stage.

The song 'Faithless Street' will always be remembered for the line 'I started this damn country band, because punk rock was too hard to sing'. It may, some day, rank alongside 'Hope I die before I get old' as a statement, and like Pete Townshend Ryan would rapidly become weary of explaining or justifying it. "People really made a big fuss about that. I was actually joking, but some people didn't take it humorously at all. You know what Americans are like. I'm an American and we have no sense of humour. 'Is punk rock *really* harder to play than country music?' It's like, shuddup. Fuck off."

In its original form, 'Angels Are Messengers From God' (titled after its first line) had borne a group credit, and that remained so here, but third time round would be attributed to Adams and Cary alone. Caitlin's fiddle was certainly the major instrumental force, duking it out with Ricker's pedal steel. She was equally prominent in the male/female vocal mix, which was pure Gram and Emmylou.

Perhaps because it was his creation alone, Ryan would take 'Mining Town' from Whiskeytown into his own solo repertoire. That said, he's gone on record as stating he hadn't cared for the song much in its Whiskeytown incarnation and only warmed to it later when stripped back to the bare guitar and vocal bones. There sounds like a glitch or two in the pedal steel, which takes the main instrumental burden behind persuasively strummed acoustics, but it all somehow adds to the ramshackle charm.

The unusual combination of Ryan and Skillet Gilmore was responsible for 'If He Can't Have You', a rowdy bar-room tearjerker in which Caitlin's fiddle had problems finding the space to be heard. 'If he can't have you, guess that no one else will' is the tenor of the lyric – and Ryan was still on a break-up kick when he penned 'Black Arrow, Bleeding Heart', a ballad to rank with *Heartbreaker*'s best.

'Matrimony' was Caitlin's stage showcase, which she wrote with a musical hand from bassist Steve Grothman. She's always preferred collaborations, reckoning the music "always comes out more complicated and interesting than I could have done by myself." Her conclusion, that 'Matrimony is misery', runs against her mother's beliefs, but she insists 'I'll use my cherry my own way'.

The final three tracks, the pizza-packet penned 'Hard Luck Story', 'Top Dollar' and 'Oklahoma', were slated by one reviewer as "bar-band knockoffs compared to what's up-front. But by then it hardly matters; it's merely the difference between a great album and a full-on classic." Significantly, 'Oklahoma', which Adams claims never to have liked and which had started life as one of the *Rural Free Delivery* tracks, would be the one and only song omitted from *Faithless Street* when the album was reissued in 1998.

But the hellraising, hard country 'Hard Luck Story', with its cliché/chuckle-ridden admission that 'I'm a fast talkin', hell-raising son of a bitch' deserves to retain its place. 'Top Dollar' is certainly worth inclusion though it's got little to do with Ryan Adams, being a Phil Wandscher showcase. He's spent all his money on a woman who's left him with nothing – sound familiar?

Nor is this the last we'd hear of Wandscher, who co-penned 'Revenge' with Ryan – The Rolling Stones-style guitar chords and burst of feedback heralding the song are probably his. But it's Adams who delivers some positively teenage lyrics with a very new-wave aplomb. Not one to remember beyond its two minutes 38, perhaps, but a noisy, bratty indication of what Whiskeytown were like live.

One reviewer was entranced by the whole. "It's plain there was a fearless new voice on the modern country-rock horizon, a young ruined throat with a vintage crack-up quality highly prized by purists. The songs seem to emerge from a beaten singer's collision course with his complacent Main Street environment, a clash from which any respite would always remain temporary. Still, the songwriter's struggle to realise the smallest romantic satisfaction against all odds seems fated."

No lyrics were made available to accompany the release – a decision, Ryan revealed, that was made for a good reason. "I just think it's up to the person listening (to interpret them)," he insisted. "I think if any of the lyrics had been written down on the inside of the record cover you would still have had less of an idea of what I truly, actually meant anyway." He evidently enjoyed keeping the listener guessing. "I can be very specific then open it up with two lines that make you go, 'What?' and that's usually because I am that way. I'm usually non-specific about my own feelings; I'm usually at the mercy of them and trying to understand them as well."

It wasn't hard to warm to *Faithless Street*, which pulled the emotional levers of country while supplying a shot or two of intoxicating rock spirit. "There's a lot of severity to the songs," Adams commented. "There's a good depressive feel to some of them, and a heart-warming feel, too. But the hopefulness definitely comes from the music, not the lyrics."

He still rated it a masterpiece a couple of years later. "I think it's a strong youth album. It's crazy. It loves what it borrows from musically: it tips its hat to Gram Parsons, it tips its hat to the Stones, it's shaking hands with Uncle Tupelo on some levels. I don't think of it as an 'inspired' record or an 'inspiring' record – I think it's both. *Faithless Street* is a proud, proud thing for me." Unusual praise from any musician for a first recording: most are usually deprecated if not disowned.

But Whiskeytown were still very much local heroes, and very likely to remain so should they continue on the road with Mood Food. All involved were now agreed their ambitions spread further than that. The album hadn't received a multitude of reviews, one typical reading: "*Faithless Street* is full of heartfelt twang, keening vocals and lyrics about such loaded American topics as baseball, beer and real hard work. The band has definitely imbibed a lot of

Bruce Springsteen and John Cougar Mellencamp, although it does try to adulterate those influences with patches of R.E.M. and The Byrds."

The 40-odd minutes that turned Whiskeytown from indie-label hopefuls to major-label contenders would be played out on March 16, 1996 in a bar called the Split Rail in Austin, Texas. Austin was that year's venue for the South by Southwest (SXSW) Music Conference, an annual showcase of talent attended by every mover and shaker worthy of their name in the world's music business. Unfortunately for the delegates, the venue for Whiskeytown's performance, the Waterloo Brewery, was so crammed that the doors were shut and people were being turned away – an almost unheard-of occurrence when the whole world and their agent had set up similar competing events.

Adams left the stage and headed back to his band's van, where a familiar bottle awaited. What he'd later term a "very sloppy set" would actually turn out to be a good night's work, for they soon found themselves the object of many labels' attentions. Three months later, after another show in Los Angeles, they finally signed up to the Outpost label, a so-called 'major indie' which had the backing of the mighty Geffen label. Outpost would make the band its third signing after Veruca Salt and Hayden.

The original talent-spotter had been Chris Stamey, the previously mentioned co-founder of Eighties power-pop outfit The dB's, who in 1993 had returned to the state of his raising and settled in Chapel Hill, not far from Raleigh. Venues there like the Cats Cradle, Local 506 and Duke Coffee House were regular band haunts, and an introduction was swiftly made. Said Stamey of his discoveries: "Whiskeytown gives me chills."

An impressed Stamey passed a copy of the album to Mark Williams, who'd started Outpost with Litt and Gershon in January 1996. Williams' major claim to fame had been signing The Smashing Pumpkins while he was vice president of A&R at Virgin, and he was clearly just as impressed with Adams and company as he'd been with Billy Corgan's band.

"It was the kind of music I've always loved," said Williams, who called Adams "the closest thing to a pure songwriter I've ever come across. If you look at the bands I worked with when I was at Virgin – Camper Van Beethoven, Cracker, The Geraldine Fibbers – I have a real affinity for dark, country-inspired rock music." For Ryan Adams, the source of so much of this kind of music, the $5,000 advance he personally obtained from the label meant he could finally afford a permanent address at which to park his record collection and single bag of ever grubbier clothes.

Since the break-up with his long-term girlfriend he'd remained deliberately rootless "because I knew no matter where I was going to actually settle my things down I would probably be pretty sad. As long as I stay moving I don't have time to think about feeling . . . I keep my stuff at a couple of different friends' houses, and when I'm on tour I just roam."

Linking to a 'real' record label and the rewards it would bring proved to be a life-changing experience. As Ryan commented optimistically soon after being signed, "We can do real band things now. When we were making *Faithless Street* our lives weren't falling apart, but we were trying to balance having a job with trying to tour and all kinds of stuff – insane shit, you know. It really put a hurt on everybody's personal life. When things finally went in the clear with Outpost, man, it was just great. We couldn't be happier."

Unfortunately, just as things should have been getting easier for Whiskeytown, they got worse. Much worse. Having ventured to nearby Durham six months after their first recording to record what they thought would be their second album with Chris Stamey producing, they presented the 19 songs cut at the 'Baseball Park Sessions' to Outpost/Geffen – only to have them rejected. Some of these would eventually surface when *Faithless Street* was reissued, while a couple – '16 Days' and 'Yesterday's News' – were considered strong enough by the powers that be to make it to their next (and first Outpost) release in re-recorded form.

"I think most people really expected (us to record) a rocking, raw, Stonesy kind of record, maybe like *Faithless Street*, but a little more into the red," Adams would explain of this still-born sophomore effort. "But there would have been no point in making that record right now. It wasn't the record we needed to make." A notoriously bad tourer, his stated intent had been to spend no more than three weeks on the road at any one time and record as much material for release as possible. But Whiskeytown's changing musical dynamic was at odds with the extensive touring cycle on which they were engaged. Spending four months making a record and touring for eight months added up to a potential problem.

Particularly when, like Ryan Adams, you had new songs coming out of your ears. But he eventually decided to cut his losses and move on. "If we had released the first 12 good songs we recorded since *Faithless Street*," he said, "we'd still be stuck in the past. We'd have ended up totally bored. So we sacrificed that record . . ."

Caitlin was less enamoured of the rock'n'roll side of the repertoire, and was beginning to show it. "I don't participate in it. I sort of stand off to the side and I actually have this feeling that I'm charmed, like nobody really associates me with that shit. And I try real hard to not be associated with it. Maybe I'm wrong, I'm sure a lot of people probably think I'm an asshole or whatever just because that stuff happens in the band that I'm in. For the most part," she concluded, "if it's loud and annoying I'm not gonna like it or choose to listen to it. But I guess at the same time I can see some of the appeal."

The band's live shows of the time were characterised by a kind of shambling amateurism. "I think that professionalism is cool but we're just normal guys, we're not trying to kid anybody," said Ryan. Criticism from purists for not being able to tune properly met with a stream of righteous indignation. "I'm the guy who's on stage. I don't ask them to come to my show. It's not about them, it's about what we're doing. I get really defensive when it comes to people coming down on the shows. Playing live is important, and you always want it to be at least entertaining . . . A lot of nights the fire starts cooking and we are just playing this amazing stuff as though we were recording it, but we've always just been the guys down the street, kicking the can, having fun, drinking beer and playing."

The second album's rejection certainly wasn't helping the line-up retain its stability. Steel guitarist Nicholas Petti had been added to the live line-up to duplicate what Bob Ricker had originated in the studio, but he failed to last longer than June 1996. Next to go was Steve Grothman, who had reservations as to the band's rockier musical direction. Suddenly, though, Whiskeytown wasn't just without a bassist – it had lost a whole rhythm section. "Skillet came in and quit that same day, two minutes later," Adams said. "About three weeks later, he asked to rejoin, and I declined him the opportunity, because I believe that, if you quit, you're gone, you don't come back."

Even Caitlin Cary, the only fixture in the Whiskeytown story alongside Ryan, came close to packing it in. "I came close to (leaving) when the first big bust happened . . . the very first one when Skillet and Steve quit. I was on the fence, totally. But no, I never actually did quit. I talked about it a lot but I stuck in there."

A band that had been held together by the centrifugal force of constant gigging was falling apart at the seams. The whole idea of playing for fun was suddenly a thing of the past. It was a money thing now, and Gilmore's sudden disillusionment would, eventually, ring a bell with Ryan when the burden of bandleading finally dulled the pleasure of music-making. "I know that, at the time, Skillet didn't like the idea that it had turned into a lot of phone calls, managers, and lawyers. I can see how he felt that way, because we were hardly ever playing."

The stability of the whole unit was under threat, and Outpost was worried enough to feature only Adams and Wandscher – ironically the best of enemies, if the perceived creative core – in a new batch of publicity pictures. It all seemed to back up Adams' earlier assertion to journalist David Menconi that "Whiskeytown is five completely different people whose main focus is to write good songs. We're not the sort of friends who hang out a lot and get real 'buddy-buddy'. This whole band is sort of an accident. If anything happens, it happens."

And that was certainly the case on stage where Menconi, the popular music critic for Raleigh's local paper, the *News & Observer* (where Ryan had once found temporary work), witnessed some memorable nights. Not that the music was always the sole factor that made them so. In 2001, he recalled the occasion Adams went missing in mid-set at the Brewery, their favourite early local haunt.

He had departed the stage, as was his custom, during Caitlin Cary's solo spot: "She used to call her song 'Matrimony' 'the Ryan interlude', because he didn't have anything to do when she sang it . . . so he would sometimes leave the stage." Popping next door, presumably to the Comet Lounge (to which the Brewery was connected and which is mentioned in the *Stranger's Almanac* song 'Yesterday's News'), he happened to fall in with a bunch of friends and totally forgot that he was due to return to work.

"He ran back," Menconi resumes, "and found the band had gone on without him; they'd run out of songs and were playing covers. So he ran to the front of the stage and started heckling them, yelling that they sucked. He told me later that there's nothing more fun than heckling your own band." The episode, Menconi concluded, showed that Adams "really understands rock mythology and how to play into it. He's *perfect* for the part of a rock star."

Caitlin Cary offered an insider's insight into the Whiskeytown live experience when she rated the chances of "a falling-apart show" as approximately 50-50. She couldn't swear that any time in the foreseeable future they would be "like The Wallflowers, a band that goes up and just does their thing. You know the kind of band I'm talking about – professional, plays the songs that are on the record and make everybody happy." But then Whiskeytown fans were used to that little something extra, and were prepared to pay for it.

The departing Gilmore would later mend his fences with the band and work as road manager on a nationwide tour, even sitting in on a couple of occasions. But Adams admits he too almost abandoned the band he'd created in favour of the easier option of singing solo. At least one offer was on the table from a major label, A&M (ironically The Flying Burrito Brothers' old record company). "Then I said, 'No, I can't give up the ship. I've worked too hard, and Whiskeytown is still a good band.' "

Certainly, one ray of light flickered through the storm clouds when they appeared as a small item on the cover of *Billboard* magazine, America's prestigious trade paper. Perhaps it was this that persuaded Caitlin Cary to hang in there. "At that particular time, she wasn't even sure what she was gonna do," Wandscher said. "She never really even knew until we went to make the new record (*Strangers Almanac*) in Nashville."

Fearful of losing out on their investment, Outpost were prepared to augment Adams and Wandscher by hiring a session bassist and drummer to play in the studio. "There was a lot of friction between me and Ryan, and there was some dramatic shit that happened at shows," Wandscher recalls. "But ultimately, that stuff made our relationship stronger, because there was a fire there to fuel every now and then. Which is sometimes pretty good – rather than nothing ever happening, and people keeping stuff inside. That . . . was never the case between me and Ryan. We would just blow up upon each other, but it was good to get all that out in the air right then and there." But the partnership was not to last.

Fast growing in confidence, Ryan had taken on much more of the guitar-playing load of late. From plugging his Les Paul straight into a Fender Twin Reverb combo 12 months earlier, he was now employing a rather more sophisticated set-up to keep pace with his burgeoning technique and confidence. "I've always felt a really competent guitar player, but never had the ability to show it," he divulged. Now, he had a veritable array of effects units – an outboard reverb box, an Echoplex tape echo and a Small Stone phaser – between his Gibson guitar and a stereo pair of Silvertone amps, though he insisted "real guitar playing is acoustic guitar playing . . . electric is like a toy."

Whether or not he felt it was 'authentic', the transition from electric to acoustic guitar was changing not only Ryan Adams' own sound but the sound of the group. "The sonics of the acoustic guitar are more tonal, not as easy to mess with as an electric. On acoustic you find yourself playing more traditional things. Open tunings sound cool. So I started incorporating these things into a band. It was a slower, fatter sound. What we were doing was not necessarily country, but a lot of it just sounded country."

As *No Depression* reflected in one of its many features on Whiskeytown: "*Faithless Street* wasn't just one of the finest début discs of the year or one of the finest alt.country albums of the year; it was one of the best records of the year . . . period." Yet when

Adams looked back at the original he was not content: "You should have heard it before it got all cut up."

It was fortunate that fans would later be given the chance to do just that when *Faithless Street* was reissued. For now, though, it was time for the band to re-group with newcomers Steve Terry and Jeff Rice on drums and bass respectively and cut another album. It was time to open the *Strangers Almanac.*

4

Nashville Bound

WHEN WHISKEYTOWN WAS transported Nashville-wards in February 1997 to record their second album, original title *Sorry I Said Goodbye*, with producer Jim Scott, it must all have seemed a long way from the (effectively) self-produced effort, cut in a barn, that had preceded it. Time and resources were now being channelled in their direction, but crucial to the plot was that Whiskeytown would not be calling the tune this time – they would be playing by major-label rules.

Outpost had made it clear, by rejecting the Stamey-produced second album (alleged to have been titled *Those Weren't The Days* but which became known, posthumously, as *The Baseball Park Sessions*), that they had a particular direction in mind for the band. "Jim was a big part of the sound of this record," said label boss Mark Williams of what would become *Strangers Almanac*. "We thought about a lot of different people and came up with him because I've always loved Tom Petty's *Wildflowers*. I sent Jim a tape, and he immediately reacted to the songwriting and to Ryan's voice. His catch phrase was, 'I *believe* him.' "

Indeed, Adams was never less than believable throughout. "I do put my ass on the line," he told *Country Music International*'s Alan Cackett. "I think, because of my age, some people will think it's a smart kid just making stuff up. But it's not that at all. Some people will like this record and get it – at least I hope they will. It will talk to people, I think."

That goal was achieved with some ease, even if he claimed – with a sly look in the direction of Outpost – that the primary goal of the band wasn't to sell records. "What we wanted to do was to be really fucking good, be really stable, be there for each other and have a cohesive unit. We wanted it to be the best rock'n'roll band that anybody'd fucking heard. There were times when we were really close."

That team spirit, though, would be tested – and in terms of recording a memorable album, they had to overcome the drawback that drummer Terry and bassist Rice had first played together as a rhythm section about a week before entering the studio. "We didn't practise to make the record. We just said, 'We're going to Nashville to make a record, are you guys ready to go?' They said all right, we got in the car, and there we were."

Steve Terry, the son of a church minister, had taken to the drums at age nine, and had grown up listening to country music despite also listing AC/DC, Mötley Crüe and Rush as influences (well, Alice Cooper was a preacher's son, too!). His take on Whiskeytown's direction was, "We're a rock'n'roll band that sounds like country," while his admiration for the frontman was whole-hearted. "Ryan's a very pure songwriter. His writing is straightforward and direct. It's very hard to say something simply, but in a way that people hearing it go 'Whoa!' He's that kind of songwriter."

Whatever image Ryan Adams and Whiskeytown had of Nashville, country's famous Music City, the reality was to prove sobering. There was clearly a clash of direction to contend with. Adams and company wanted to make "cool indie records", while their label "wanted to make us famous". The first three days of pre-recording rehearsal were scarcely better. "I thought (Jim Scott) was gonna cry, because we sounded like shit. We sounded *horrible*."

Further problems were to follow, as producer Scott proved a far harder taskmaster than they had been used to. Adams' preference for first takes clashed head-on with the experienced producer's perfectionist tendencies. "He's like, 'Quit jerkin' me.' That was his line the whole time: 'Are you gonna play something good, or are you gonna jerk me?' We jerked him for about a month, and then we finally did some good takes."

In retrospect, Adams has some sympathy with the producer. "I think he loved the demos and the stuff we had going on before we went in to make the record. But by the time we got in to make it, so much of what we'd been had fallen apart that I think he felt he was literally working with nothing." Caitlin Cary was initially taken aback by Scott's straight talking, then learned to appreciate it. "Jim was very candid about which performance was the performance. And we all learned to trust him when he said, 'That was *it*.' "

There was a less easy compromise reached between Scott's desire to use the highest possible technology and Adams' preference for tube (valve) equipment over modern transistors. Fellow guitarist Wandscher sided with Scott, and enjoyed experimenting with a variety of amps and effects to come up with new sounds, though Cary, like Adams, lamented the lack of spontaneity in the recording process – the more so because the majority of her contributions were overdubbed from the control room rather than playing with the 'core' band in the studio proper.

Depressed with the turn events were taking, Adams would leave the Woodland Studios complex, situated in a poor black area of Nashville, to buy bottles of Southern Comfort, and "commenced getting trashed as hell walkin' down the strip, with a bottle of liquor in a brown bag. I was lost . . . I needed to go walk down the street, feel something, feel alive. Because I'd been confined in the studio. So I come back, and I had been in the shit. And now I knew where I was."

There was, it transpired, a reason for him finding solace in Janis Joplin's favourite tipple "which makes it a wonder", he later admitted, "that I got out of my early twenties." He was unhappy "with *everything* . . . I'd lost my girlfriend, the house we'd stayed in, records, guitars, all kinds of shit. And all that came out in the studio." To make matters worse, the room he was staying in didn't have a light that worked, Adams existing off-duty by the flickering shadows cast by the TV. "I just sat, drank and watched the tube."

A contemporary press release for the album confirms that this indeed was "an 'it's over' record. It's a romantic split-up album, but a lot of other things were going on too. Skillet and Steve had left, and our lives had changed a lot because of the band. Almost all the songs on the record are about loss."

He'd indeed split with the partner he'd been living with for the past two and a half years and, with the loss of two key band members to deal with on top of that, it was clear his mental state was fragile. By the time of *Strangers Almanac* Adams admits he was "like an egg being carried around in a cement pocket. People were being really careful with me because I was about to crack. All that strangeness and oddity in my life, how terrible it was, that whole year, it started in anger and ended in grief. It ended with me being fragile, drained physically, emotionally, and even musically."

Added to this, he retained the chip on his shoulder that Outpost hadn't allowed the *Baseball Park Sessions* to be released. Even in late 2001, Adams would recall his resentment and would complain that the process of recording *Strangers Almanac* "killed the band". Ironically, he'd return to the same studio three years later and cut his first solo album, *Heartbreaker*, in just 11 days, compared with the four weeks recording and three weeks mixing the band effort would require.

With antipathy and alienation rife in the studio and elsewhere, it was amazing that what emerged musically should have been so worthwhile (even Ryan calling it a "fun, groovy album"). It's reckoned that something approaching three dozen songs were committed to tape, only 13 of which would make the final cut. The result, according to *Magnet* magazine, was "a rock album with overt country references that drew as much from the Fleetwood Mac playbook as from (Gram) Parsons." Interestingly, from that writer's point of view, Whiskeytown were now clearly a rock band.

And if they were looking for inspiration in that regard, they needed look no further than across the corridor where The Rolling Stones were ensconced recording their umpteenth album, *Bridges To Babylon*. The band Adams credited as "part of the mythology of our generation" seemed to keep much the same hours as Whiskeytown, both outfits' working days starting in the early evening, and Ryan started rubbing shoulders with Keith Richards – literally – on the narrow stairwell leading up to the studio toilet.

But this friendly friction would become somewhat more incendiary, and sparks flew when an incident erupted between Keith and Phil Wandscher which led to the Stone chasing Adams' guitar partner down the hall with a vodka bottle in his hand. Ryan, who wasn't there when the event went down, laughed it off, though he was less amused when, in Chinese whisper fashion, it would change round to become a tale in which Richards had wanted to kill *him*. "I think Charlie got snubbed in front of Keith," he commented. "It was accidental, and it set Keith off." Certainly, the image of the Stone swigging from the ever-present vodka bottle and Adams matching him slug for slug on the Southern Comfort is an interesting one.

Ryan had never seen the Stones, but hit it off with Charlie Watts to the extent that he agreed to bring his fellow band members with him to see Whiskeytown live. A dozen seats were reserved at a Toronto gig, "roped off with gold cord, but nobody showed."

The introduction had come via one Ethan Johns, one of the younger movers and shakers on the Nashville scene. He was the son of Glyn Johns, the engineer/producer who'd worked with the Stones and indeed The Who, Steve Miller and Rod Stewart in a long career. Superintending The Eagles' first recordings had seen him gain particular fame in the States, hence the subsequent re-location, and Ethan, who was following in his father's footsteps as well as establishing a reputation as a talented multi-instrumentalist, was in another of the complex's studios working with Stephen Stills' son Chris. Both Johns and Stills would be names that would recur in the Ryan Adams story.

More immediately, though, a guy called John Ginty would be contributing piano, Wurlitzer electric piano and Hammond organ to Whiskeytown's sophomore long-player. Interestingly, the New Jersey native had been drawn to the keyboard through enjoying southern rock bands like The Allman Brothers. He became Neal Casal's keyboardist in 1993 but his ability to play tastefully and with texture saw him called upon to play many sessions: Whiskeytown was one of these.

Also on the team was pedal steel player Greg Leisz (pronounced Lees), who combined knowledge of the country genre with a degree of stylistic open-mindedness rare among his breed. Older than his studio compadres but sharing their irreverent outlook, Leisz had spent his formative years catching seminal acts like The Byrds and The Flying Burrito Brothers in the clubs of Southern

California. Determined not to let himself be pigeonholed as just a roots musician, Leisz took gigs outside the Nashville mainstream, in every case looking to add to a song rather than place his own mark all over it. By the end of the millennium, his client list would include such luminaries as Sheryl Crow, Joni Mitchell, kd lang, Wilco and Lucinda Williams.

Additional musicians included Kirk Bisquera on percussion and Rick Latina, whose pedal steel guitar appeared solely on '16 Days', pegging the track as an earlier effort. The Pocket Horns (Dan Navarro on trumpet, Crecencio Gonzalez on trombone and Jim Goodwin on alto sax) also featured, while producer Scott added a little percussion to the mix when the fancy took him.

After the band credits on *Faithless Street*, *Strangers Almanac* was presented from the outset as very much an Adams creation. Four songs bore a Wandscher co-credit, Cary chipping in on a further one. "The whole band sings," explained Ryan, "but Caitlin and Phil don't actually take any of their own songs on this next record. It's mostly like all my record, this is sort of an exorcism record for me. I really needed to write this record to feel better."

With such an accent on his songs, it was tempting to think the next stage would be Ryan Adams and Whiskeytown. Not so, he claimed. "I don't really lead this band, that's not my mission. This record has all my songs on it, but it's just that nobody in the band had written any in that period. This next record, Caitlin will probably have a couple, and Phil will probably contribute three or four."

Their current reticence, he claimed, was due to the pressures they'd seen him under. "I think those guys are reluctant to step into the spotlight because they're realising how extremely tough it is on somebody. It's not easy to be up there and be looked at like that – especially because we had different ideas when we started the band. When we started, we assumed a shared limelight. Now, it falls mostly on me.

"I didn't ask for it, it just kind of happened. It's a weird thing, but there's no jealousy in the band from it, because they don't want it and know I don't either. They've got it a little easier, though. Not much, because they have to deal with my shit dealing with it, which is probably worse. It just makes me more scared and apprehensive about what I'm doing and how to do it." The task was daunting, but he wasn't going to duck it. "A lot of times you just have to step up there and say, 'All right, if the spotlight is going to fall on me, I'm going to take the ball and run with it, fuck it.' It's better than standing there and saying, 'I don't want to play this game.' "

And when it came down to the game of writing songs, the man was clearly on top form. *Strangers Almanac* kicked off with 'Inn Town', a typical Ryan Adams bar-stool character sketch with snakily winding three-part harmonies from Adams, Cary and Wandscher. Paul Sexton of *The (*London*) Times* enjoyed the fact that the opening "coy acoustic guitar seems to put them in James Taylor territory: then in comes a country fiddle and we adjust their imagined locale to a boots-and-Stetsons bar-room." *Country Music International*'s Tim Perry also saluted "a minute of magic . . . but the beauty soon wears off and the idea doesn't stand up to another five minutes' worth."

But if that was impressive (to most listeners, anyway), 'Excuse Me While I Break My Own Heart Tonight' had an unpredictable twist on board in the shape of Alejandro Escovedo, once of country-rockers Rank and File, who took a second lead vocal on the song's last verse to take it into another dimension. (Ryan had met Austin-based Escovedo in Austin at the SXSW event.) Equally cover-worthy by the likes of the Stones or The Mavericks, it was the first of three tracks on which he'd feature, though sadly this time Caitlin would not be accorded a vocal showcase of her own.

Having established a mood, it was a pity the heavy-guitar intro of 'Yesterday's News' (like the album opener an Adams/Wandscher collaboration) came along to break it in sledgehammer fashion. But the song would prove an effective introduction to Whiskeytown for many when it was released on its own.

'16 Days' would also be extracted as a single, but could hardly have been more different. This was accurately pinpointed by one reviewer as Ryan's take on Gram Parsons' 'Return Of The Grievous Angel', with its lines about 'a bottle and a rosary/I owe you an apology.' In the words of another, it "combined a manly vulnerability with a nice poetic flourish", and certainly the re-appearance of Caitlin's harmonies made the listener realise how important these were to the appeal of the whole.

Mention should be made here of the single's non-album B-side, 'Wither, I'm A Flower', which caught an influential ear in the movie business and found a place on the soundtrack for the Harry Connick Jr/Sandra Bullock movie *Hope Floats* alongside the far better-known likes of Sheryl Crow, The Rolling Stones, Lyle Lovett, Deana Carter and Trisha Yearwood.

Subtitled (Miss You) in brackets, 'Everything I Do' cheekily borrowed its title from Ryan's near-namesake's record-breaking hit from 1991. *Country Music International* rated it "a country-soul vibe straight out of Muscle Shoals", and there were certainly echoes of the Burritos' take on the classic 'Dark End Of The Street'. Then again, the combination of co-writer Wandscher's fluid guitar licks and organ screamed Rolling Stones circa 'Angie'. A demo version that's since circulated features different guitar parts and a vocal role for Caitlin, but Jim Scott's production regime called for much revision. Something that happily survived, though, were Ryan's emotion-laden vocals.

Leading in with lilting violin, 'Houses On The Hill' – written by Ryan and Caitlin – was somewhat reminiscent of 'The Old Soft Shoe' on Gram Parsons' *GP*. The lyric was one of Adams' most realised creations to date, talking of a woman whose lover was sent to war and never returned; he is going through her memorabilia in the attic. The song developed from an acoustic demo with violin to a fuller arrangement utilising John Ginty's piano skills and is one many fans have pinpointed as a Whiskeytown classic. It's a song that shows great maturity from a young man who could only have been 22 at the time he wrote it.

Ryan's love of mid-Seventies vintage Fleetwood Mac had been showing up in Whiskeytown's live shows via a countrified version of their *Rumours* standout 'Dreams'. Rather than recording a straight cover, Whiskeytown applied the treatment to 'Turn Around'. Again, Caitlin Cary had a hand in the writing, and this was a track that, had it been released as a single by a bigger-name band, could easily have made a mark. Production, however, was not the greatest with fuzzy effects and a strange guitar introduction; the comparatively basic demo version is worth catching.

'Dancing With The Women At The Bar' seemed very autobiographical in its lyric, and was certainly the most impressive narrative on offer. Adams was well aware of the dangers of being too revealing: "It's almost like hearing someone read pages for a diary, it can be semi-embarrassing . . . that's part of the reason we beat it up with trashy guitars."

Notwithstanding that, this was one of the few Whiskeytown songs he'd play in his early solo sets, so it must have represented something special to him. At the forefront here was the steel guitar of Greg Leisz, whose haunting licks could have been lifted from a George Jones album.

'Waiting To Derail' was a song that Adams admitted showed its lineage when played live, when "it sounds exactly like Hüsker Dü". It pounds along like a locomotive out of control in studio form, too, with call and response vocals from the guitarists that add to the intensity. All the same, more of a live staple than one to put on repeat play.

By complete contrast comes 'Avenues', a track which "wouldn't have sounded out of place on Paul Westerberg's last solo album" according to one reviewer, which addressed the dilemma of living in close proximity to an ex-love but having to forget their very existence. Subtle piano and Hammond organ add colour to a song delivered slackly against slap-back acoustic guitar in a style bringing to mind Scots singer-songwriter John Martyn.

'Losering' was a really easy song to create and, to Ryan, was emblematic of how the record as a whole "became its own entity, beyond us." John Ginty accidentally hit the piano in the background of the song which merged with an existing chord to make an unidentifiable but captivating sound. "You want to say it's a dulcimer, then you think it's a twin fiddle, but you don't know."

'Somebody Remembers The Rose' was the album's final Adams/Wandscher collaboration and arguably their strongest ever. Unusually bereft of howling electric lead, it rode comfortably along on a mix of piano and subtly picked country guitar. The lyric was a simple but effective reflection on lost love. And though there was no love lost between the co-writers, Phil would join a solo Ryan on stage in February 2001 to reprise the number.

Final track 'Not Home Anymore' (also known as 'You're Gone') was also the album's longest – and arguably bleakest. Since Ryan has described *Strangers Almanac* as "13 songs about loss", then this is surely the one to send you towards the abyss. A funereal fiddle over an insistent drumbeat ushered in an Adams vocal that made hairs rise on the back of the neck. Then answering vocals made themselves felt in a back and forth conversation. The overall effect, with scratchy echoed guitar punctuating his phrases, was reminiscent of British folk-rock band Fairport Convention in their Richard Thompson period. And that's high praise indeed. Atonal guitars played out a bittersweet tale of betrayal that didn't outstay its welcome.

To sum up, *Strangers Almanac* was a mature work that more than lived up to the promise of earlier releases. Though songs had been recorded in a wide range of styles, most of the tunes to make the final cut were quiet and understated, creating something of an intense mood. The album's slow pace would have come as a surprise to those familiar with the often raucous live shows, but tilting the album toward Whiskeytown's quieter side was a conscious decision.

Country Music International, a rare dissenting voice, suggested the album "smacked of a major label trying to achieve crossover potential with an exciting young band before the time was right" (echoing Ryan's own accusations that their label "wanted to make us famous"), while the *Guardian* suggested Whiskeytown had "borrowed wolfishly from the entire spectrum of rugged Americana without forging anything distinctly their own." Certainly, Ryan's magpie songwriting tendencies were not hard to discern.

Guardian reviewer Tom Cox had another go in *New Musical Express*, which gave him more column inches to develop his argument. His suggestion was that "at 23 Adams is too young to have seen the world so he interprets the one witnessed by older artists instead. And, permeated with this bedraggled second-hand emotion, *Strangers Almanac* could never be more than a reassuring truckstop on alternative country's journey to a Nirvana-style breakthrough."

The successful completion of *Strangers Almanac* led to a five-piece Whiskeytown photo session. Adams and Wandscher sat astride the trunk of a gloriously be-finned (but far from showroom-new) American car parked in a field, with Cary hanging out of the passenger window. Another had the five sat at a bar, beers set up in front of them as (almost) befitted their name.

But Ryan Adams had not come out of the experience with any kind of satisfaction. An interview with *Country Music International*'s Sally O'Shaughnessy found him outlining future plans in expansive manner while damning the whole hit-making machinery as he did so. "It was horrible working in Nashville," he moaned. "Nashville's a *terrible* place. Even the pictures lie. It's this fake thing that used to be Music City, USA . . . I was being disappointed by the town every day and making a record I had no control over.

"The next record," he insisted, "will be a double album – and I'm going to make sure I produce this one." He also claimed that if *Strangers Almanac* was "a pissed-off, scared album, I've got a worse one on the way. You ain't seen shit yet."

The fact was that a name producer and increased production values added a gloss that cynics could read as selling out. "In some ways, it must seem strategic as fuck," Adams conceded, "but I think we made a really cool, really smart record. And I don't think there's anything bad about us making a kind of really cheesy-sounding record." He cited *Don't Tell A Soul* by The Replacements as an example of a cool album by a cool band which survived the production upgrade process. "The producer of that record, Matt Wallace, stepped in and said, 'Listen boys, we know what you can do lo-fi and we know what you can do strung out, because you've been that way for eight years. But we're going to make you sound good now.' It's proof you can have a record sound really great and still be cool guys in a cool band."

But the fact remained that he hadn't seen eye to eye with Jim Scott over several matters, Adams admitting there had been faults on his own side. Differences of opinion had arisen over his guitar playing, while getting him to sing had been "like pulling teeth because I was completely depressed. I was a mess . . . really bad. Even if we work with Jim Scott again," he insisted, "the difference will be the availability of that huge sound, but I'll have really compressed guitars. I'll have feedback. I'll let it breathe. Do whatever it is we do live." Whatever happened, he was already itching to get on to the next project. "I'm 23 years old, and I have a lot of records to make," Adams says. "And I'm going to be persistent about making them, whether or not they actually get put out."

If he was keen to represent more of Whiskeytown's raw live side, then the CD EP/mini album *Rural Free Delivery*, released just two months before *Almanac* in May 1997, certainly had that in spades. Recorded in the band's first months, it consisted of early tracks plus demos the band had cut for their début album: 'Oklahoma' and 'Angels' actually made it to the finished record, the latter as title track 'Faithless Street'. The EP comprised eight named songs plus a hidden bonus. Whiskeytown were, at the point this was recorded, a baby band, having existed for a matter of weeks but, especially in retrospect, there were many signs of the greatness to come.

A countrified cover of punk band Black Flag's 'Nervous Breakdown', the lyrics delivered dead straight, contrasted with originals like the tearjerking 'Pawn Shop Ain't No Place For A Wedding Ring' and 'Take Your Guns To Town', the latter convincing enough to be hailed by *No Depression* as "maybe the definitive recording of this version of Whiskeytown."

The bonus track, another version of 'Nervous Breakdown', was located by pressing 'play' then 'reverse searching' until minus three minutes and 30 seconds of track one was reached. Mark Cimerro, who mixed *Rural Free Delivery* and is a friend of Adams, would later reveal that the pair had a disagreement when they were putting the CD together. Ryan wanted to have 'Nervous Breakdown' as a hidden track only but Mark thought the song was their "most commercial" or "most radio friendly" song and should not be concealed. It seems the non-hidden 'Nervous Breakdown' was a last-minute inclusion, but the original version was also left on there. Quite why they should be different has never been explained – nor who revealed the elaborate means of accessing it.

Mood Food were entitled to release this EP (or mini-album, if you're quibbling) as part of the payoff that had let Outpost cut the band's ties with their first label. Whiskeytown were by no means happy it appeared, but they had no real need to be upset. Because, in *No Depression*'s wise words: "Ryan Adams just plain doesn't make bad music."

If recording *Strangers Almanac* had been a fraught affair, then touring to promote it (as Outpost not unreasonably demanded) was to prove the beginning of the end for Whiskeytown. Many of the less positive stories about Ryan Adams emanate from this period as relationships between band members unravelled in the most public of ways.

It would prove a bumpy ride taking Whiskeytown out of their environment where they'd ruled the roost as the local band most likely to, and have them win over a typical alt.country punter – what their tour manager Tom O'Keefe somewhat disparagingly called "a redneck in a Son Volt hat with a bottle of Bud in his hand."

O'Keefe would mastermind no fewer than nine Whiskeytown tours in the four years from 1995, and fingers Adams' distaste for the road as the spark that would light the powder keg of Whiskeytown's destruction. "None of the tours lasted longer than five weeks," he'd explain. "That was our limit. Ryan gets bored easily and couldn't tour for five weeks without a complete meltdown – that's when the bad shit happened."

Musically, Whiskeytown were taking *Strangers Almanac*, grabbing it by its collar and giving it a good shaking. "We have to present the record as a live record, so it's much more 'Stonesy', or it sounds a lot more in the vein of *Faithless Street*." This is backed up by a number of bootleg recordings of the time.

Ryan Adams was now promoting *Strangers Almanac* as part of the master plan. "Making the kind of record we just did will probably be really good, because now things can only go backwards – back to simpler recordings, more live in the room recordings, more obscure songs, or songs that we feel are influenced by obscure artists. . . . It's easier now to go do whatever the hell we want. We did what we wanted this time, too, but now we can continue that, and it just happened that what we wanted to do with this record was make a pretty big-sounding record."

Whiskeytown's live line-up was now to be augmented by the multi-talented Mike Daly, fresh from backing Amy Rigby and

Edith Frost, whose ability to cover keyboards, lap steel and guitar (plus sundry other instruments) made him an ideal team player. Daly would later recall being introduced to the band in a very informal fashion in June 1997, the month before *Strangers*' US release. Having flown from New York City to North Carolina, he was somewhat disconcerted to find Ryan was out of town, "taking care of some business" in Austin, where he would soon choose to make his home. Nevertheless, Phil Wandscher made him most welcome by inviting him on a fishing trip for which swimming trunks had to be purchased (there being little call for them in New York).

And it was back in the Big Apple the following week that he'd found himself introduced to the rest of the band, backstage at a club called Tramps. "It was kind of a handshake: 'This is Mike, he's a fuckin' great player,' then I walked on stage and did the show." The gig was a support set to Cracker, the then-popular country-flavoured Camper van Beethoven spin-off band, and it was fortunate that Daly was a competent enough musician to "make up my parts as we went along". He would later aver that he "had my musical shit way more together than they did at that point," but his introduction was a significant step in upping the musicianship of the band in line with the quality of the songs they played.

Yet Whiskeytown's non-stop touring had a distinct dampening effect on morale. If the music produced had all the ragged glory of old, the demands of the every day/every night grind, Adams now admits, saw behaviour degenerate at times into a kind of country-rock *Spinal Tap*. Fans could never be certain which version of Whiskeytown was going to hit the stage on any given night.

One fan saw them in San Francisco "when Ryan was so hungover that they had to turn off the hot stage lights so he wouldn't pass out . . . I also caught them in Austin, Texas, when Ryan, drunk, broke two strings and then smashed his guitar. I've also seen them play with such heart and drive that I have scrawled in my notebook, 'Whiskeytown will save rock-and-roll from its pre-millennial doldrums.'"

Ryan was clearly beginning to find the pressure of being the frontman intolerable. But whenever he contemplated breaking up

Whiskeytown and embarking on a solo career, "there would be people telling me to give it another shot. And I bent over as far backwards as I could."

The singer's increasingly erratic behaviour certainly backed up road manager Mike O'Keefe's comments about him "not caring one lick for touring". The mental strain found physical outlet when he started having panic attacks on stage and, after one show, "woke up wearing an oxygen mask in the back of an ambulance." It would also become apparent that this seemingly natural performer had been suffering from chronic stage fright – a condition that reportedly used to require two Long Island ice tea cocktails and 12 beers to defeat.

One night in June 1997, at a small club, Mac's Bar, in East Lansing, Michigan, Ryan became increasingly stressed out about a soundman who, he felt, was not up to his job. This resulted in a foreshortened set and much verbal abuse of the audience. They'd hit town with rave reviews from *Rolling Stone* and *Spin* in hand only to find they were booked to play a bar populated by college students. What happened next will forever remain in dispute. Fans who arrived eager to catch the 'alt.country Nirvana' claimed they got a half-hour, half-baked performance and a "verbal middle finger" from Adams at night's end. They were offended that Whiskeytown slagged off their venue, and indeed one disgruntled fan pitched tomatoes at the band's crew as they packed up equipment.

According to Adams, he and his road-weary colleagues had been treated poorly by club staff and understandably wound up in a miserable mood, running through their set and simply telling the crowd they were "humiliated playing here". The incident blew up in the local music press, the Internet spreading the message that Adams was an impetuous jerk, his fellow band members prima donnas.

Adams wrote privately to five fans, apologising for the affair. "They said I was whiny about playing a sports bar," he's said. "You know what? I don't care who else was cool enough to play there. I'm cool enough to *not* want to play there, because I wasn't comfortable with it." He didn't, however, see their point of view. "I suppose a lot of (the Mac's audience) went to see their favourite band and it turned into a band that they hated. I can't blame them for that, but that was honestly one of the times when there was so much pressure on us as a band and on me that I think it got to be too much."

Nor did the bickering and infighting restrict itself to the stage as he put local radio stations' DJs' backs up. The single '16 Days' seemed likely to help get the name of Whiskeytown around when it was released to radio. But the meet and greeting involved in cosying up to the pilots of the airwaves didn't come naturally to Adams, who confessed he might sometimes have 'fucked it up on purpose'.

"For instance, I told the programmer in Seattle who was responsible for three major radio stations in the West to go fuck himself, and dared him to take our record off the air, which he did," Ryan admitted. "That song had been doing great, and then it was like, 'See ya,' and we were gone, over."

The scenario repeated itself in Denver, Colorado, where Ryan and Caitlin showed up to do an acoustic set and a performance of the current single was requested. Having been a month on the road, the duo's voices were showing signs of wear and tear and, with the key of the song being particularly challenging, an alternative was suggested. Instead, the DJ said, "If you don't play '16 Days' I don't want you to do anything at all." Little did he realise the response he'd get . . .

"I wasn't going in there firing off guns," Adams emphasised. "I went in there with the utmost civility and respect . . . But we had a sold-out show. Am I gonna go in there and blow my voice and let down all those people that paid money? Radio is becoming one of the most disgusting things I'm finding out about this business. It's really disappointing because you think they're into your music. But they're not. A lot of it has to do with their quest for cash." Needless to say, the episode ended in tears.

The atmosphere was somewhat different when Ryan and Caitlin jumped a jumbo and made their first visit to England. Their host was Bob Harris, the former Radio 1 disc jockey who'd also hosted TV's influential *Old Grey Whistle Test*. He'd spent the decade since hopping between a series of local radio stations, making his way slowly back up the greasy pole, and had ended up at Greater London Radio. This had a tradition of pioneering new music, first fostered (as Radio London) by Charlie Gillett in the Seventies, and Harris was happy to carry it on via live sessions in the studio. Logistics dictated this was usually smaller groups, so the duo format was ideal.

Harris had come across Ryan's music through *Strangers Almanac*, "particularly '16 Days', which I thought was fantastic. Soon after hearing that, he came into London with Caitlin, came into the show I was doing on GLR and did a session for me. It was the first and so far only time I've met him."

The session went well, but Harris detected a certain distance or reserve. "You get the impression with Ryan of somebody completely in a world of his own. He had notebooks with him – quite a few, two or three – two of which were open within minutes of him arriving. He was actually jotting down almost while talking. But it's difficult (to form a relationship with an artist) because you've only got 25–30 minutes. You're in the studio, they're playing live, you're already on air and you haven't had a chance to chat beforehand so you're only getting the most surface of impressions. But they came over as a cohesive bubble, if you like. There was this other worldliness. They came into the studio almost self contained.

"He and Caitlin did two songs – I can't remember which they were, it was about six years ago, but one of them would have been '16 Days'. As I say, he referred to notes, and then there was some discussion between him and Caitlin as to what they were going to play. They were both absolutely wonderful and I must say I became a big fan of Caitlin at that time as well."

Harris characterised the working relationship between the two performers as "a fantastic rapport. The impression I got from Caitlin was of . . . a mother who's prepared as it were to indulge her offspring, it was kind of like that. He was so interesting, though I felt there were so many layers there that you'd have to get to know him for a long time to unpeel them one by one."

Whiskeytown had suffered many personnel changes over the months they'd been together, but the key triumvirate of Adams,

Cary and Wandscher had always remained constant. It seems the turbulent summer of '97 had loosened the glue to a crucial extent. After a legendary Kansas City show in September, the guitarists – who, Cary says, were like "oil and water" – finally parted ways, and the band's rhythm section went with Wandscher.

Mike Daly recalled Adams as "freaking out" in the middle of the set, turning around in the middle of a song and announcing that he was leaving the band. If Adams was hoping Daly would stop and try to talk him out of it, he was mistaken. "I wasn't quite following him, so I asked him if that meant we were still gonna play 'Waiting To Derail' or not. Clearly that wasn't the answer he was looking for . . ."

But Adams was looking for something he wasn't going to find in present company. Tour manager O'Keefe recalls the catalyst being the new song 'Jacksonville Skyline' (which would later be released on *Pneumonia*). Its lyrics were changed to incorporate a stream of invective about specific aspects of the music business Ryan didn't like. "He finally ended the song, smashed up his guitar, grabbed the mic and told a rather stunned audience, 'Get on the Internet and tell your friends you just saw the last fuckin' Whiskeytown show.' "

Adams recalls the last days of this Whiskeytown incarnation's final fling: "We finished the last record and the tour fizzled out. If someone wasn't quitting or being fired, they were fucking going to drug rehab or having nervous breakdowns or throwing shit at you on the bus. Or there'd be times when everything would get good and we're all excited . . . then the show would suck, or whatever. It just didn't work. It should have showed us.

"One day I just stopped and said, 'Fuck this. No more. Forget it.' We should have stopped a long fucking time ago. I don't know what we were trying to do. We just bit off more than we could chew. We weren't able to . . . win at that rock'n'roll game. It just didn't fly."

The first many knew of the band's sundering was when *No Depression* sent reporter Grant Alden to review Whiskeytown at Nashville's Exit/In towards the end of September 1997. He reported a handwritten sign at the door announcing that Whiskeytown would be playing an acoustic set, "and though rumours swirled among the few there not to bask in the execrable mediocrity of opener Neal Coty, it was not entirely clear what that meant until Caitlin Cary and Ryan Adams took the stage unescorted. (It was) their second night, they said later, as a duo."

The absence of fellow band members would remain unexplained on the night. But Cary and Adams "carried off a set of songs that went on and on and on until the bar stopped serving." According to Alden, who'd witnessed some "pleasant but somehow perfunctory rock shows" a few weeks earlier in Atlanta and Knoxville, it was a case of "less is more" as the pair turned in a "powerfully vulnerable performance." Few tracks from *Strangers Almanac* were performed, as Adams reached back to the early days for 'My Heart Is Broken', a track released as a one-off Bloodshot single.

What had actually transpired was that, after the Kansas City gig, Adams had sent everyone but Cary home – soundman included – in the minibus road-manager O'Keefe had rented on his American Express card. O'Keefe, Adams and Cary had then decamped in the equipment van and played the final four dates of the tour acoustically.

In an interview with website *9X*, Adams gave some of the background to the continuous feud with his fellow guitarist that would lead to Wandscher's departure. "I think you reflect the people you're around. I was becoming a person I didn't like. I was dealing with people I didn't necessarily like any more in the former band. Steve Terry might as well have been a stranger . . . we never got to know each other. Steve took me to his house in West Virginia one time with Phil, which turned into a nightmare . . . I was trying to eat dinner with Steve Terry's parents and the whole time Phil's trying to make an ass of me."

While appreciating his talents as a guitar player, Adams found it hard to deal with Wandscher's self-confidence. "He had the sharpest tongue I've ever met. Phil could turn you *that* big (indicates an inch) in a second. Insensitive as hell. And just as manipulative." He'd later elaborate – just – to the *New York Times*. "The rumour is I fired him, but actually, we had to quit playing together. We were going to kill each other. It was a total Noel and Liam (Gallagher) kind of thing.

"You get into an abusive (band) relationship and it's easy to laugh it off: 'Oh, Keith and Mick did this, Bob (Mould) and Grant (Hart, Hüsker Dü) did this,'" he says. "But you don't have to do that, to get into stuff that doesn't have anything to do with the chords in a song. It doesn't make for good press or a good story. It just ruins lives." Cary: "Ryan and Phil had a very sick relationship, it was fucked up and terrible with big arguments, fist fights and all that."

It may not have helped that the financial rewards of their labours so far had yet to manifest themselves. In an early 1998 interview six months after the release of *Strangers Almanac*, Adams was suggesting 80,000 records had been shipped but money was, as ever in these cases, slow in trickling down to those who created the music.

In any event, he was clearly relieved the long-standing feud was over. "The going joke is that I fired them all, but I really didn't want to play with Phil Wandscher any more. Did you ever hear of a death cocktail? We were like that, mixing liquors until something died. Either one of us alone was just fine. Get us together, and whoa! We'd had a lot of fist fights in the van between me and him. I was sick of it. I was about to have a nervous breakdown, and I don't know what he was going to do."

The seeming death of Whiskeytown made headlines, if scarcely of national proportions. But while the duo at its heart, Caitlin Cary and Ryan Adams, remained together, the funeral was on hold. And if the end was inevitable, the wake would be nothing less than entertaining.

5

The Decline & Fall

WITH WHISKEYTOWN DOWN to a duo mere weeks after the release of their 'breakthrough' second album, the future was less certain than ever. It seemed as easy to carry on as to go back, however, so autumn dates would be fulfilled by Adams, Cary and four band members – two of whom were familiar names. Utility man Mike Daly was re-hired, Skillet Gilmore returned as drummer ("It's nice to have my Charlie Watts back," Adams quipped) while Jenni Snyder and ex-fIREHOSE man Ed Crawford, who'd teamed up in Grand National, came on board playing bass and guitar respectively. The latter, "a born player" according to Ryan, was very much a pupil of the Stones-y school of riffing and slotted remarkably easily into Phil Wandscher's shoes. "I feel as if I'm playing with friends," said Ryan. "I don't feel like I'm on the stage alone any more."

While much of the material was familiar, the new line-up offered a huge musical contrast from other shows Whiskeytown had played, as Ryan explained in the *Austin Chronicle*: "In the past, we have been an unsuccessful live band, a disaster – and, for the most part, we didn't care, because we were just doing things our way. But lately our shows are much more precise. We've developed live, so to speak."

Reviews of their gigs were uniformly favourable, the *Los Angeles Times* enthusing about a "set that was never less than musically stellar, and the touring sextet . . . displayed both chops and camaraderie while nimbly negotiating honky-tonk twang, punk-pop and good old rock'n'roll." Long-time fans may have missed the rough edges, but this configuration was far more likely to win over the uncommitted than the sometimes ramshackle outfit of old. Yet one voice in the ranks sounded just a little out of key with the current direction.

From on-stage appearances, it may have seemed Caitlin was relishing her career as a 'country-rock chick', but in fact she was already looking forward to a post-Whiskeytown future. "I have a feeling there'll come a day when I'll say to Ryan, 'Look, I want to do acoustic shows with you only.' I've got the rock in me for a while, I can do it and have fun with it, but that's not my ultimate goal, to be in a rock band. I would much rather lean harder on the country side or the acoustic side. I don't want to be deaf. It is a concern.

"It's fun to make any kind of records, going out and touring them for two-and-a-half years might be a different story. But I'm having fun with it now, that's about what I would say on that. I have something up my sleeve. I want to make a record of the kind of music that I want to do and I've got some songs and a lot of people who are anxious to play with me. I'll get to do my thing. And I think that people might look forward to that . . ."

The newly reconfigured band continued to tour through to the end of 1997, with Ryan seemingly making redoubled efforts to clean up his act. With a reduction in alcohol intake had come a raising of standards, he explained. "We finally have the perfect line-up and have learned how to play to audiences – plus, I don't have to get nearly as fucked-up to do it."

The 'new' Whiskeytown also recorded 11 or 12 songs "just for the hell of it", and several of these songs débuted on this tour. The "dark and moody sound" of *Strangers*, Adams said, was giving way to something more upbeat, "not so damn serious. We stretch out at our live shows. You can hear Sonic Youth, The Replacements, The Rolling Stones in the music. It's the tightest, most intense sound we've ever had. It's developing. There's a good chance this band is going to be around for a long time." Sadly, this optimism would prove unfounded since, a few months after this interview, Crawford, Snyder and Gilmore had all departed the ranks.

Still, it was fun while it lasted. Adams was clearly enjoying himself more as part of the new line-up, and was quoted as saying that a nine-date mini-tour in harness with Fastball in early 1998 was Whiskeytown's best ever up to that point. When the pressure built, his way out was not so much resorting to recreational drugs but to head back to Jacksonville and hang out with Alan, a childhood buddy. "I'll go in the back yard and chop wood or rake the leaves. Do something (that's) not music. Then we'll sit around, and we'll pick guitars; at night-time, over some beers or watch some TV . . . it's natural or normal."

He was also widening his musical worldview beyond the confines of Whiskeytown. Among several side projects under consideration was a collaboration with Tommy Stinson of The Replacements, who'd invited him to record with him in LA. The other candidate was Neko Case, a Canadian alt.country singer who'd found some success on the Bloodshot label. She had a voice, he explained, that "sounds like what the epitome of what singing is. It comes right out of her and makes your spine contort."

He was planning to record a full album with Case, but the only collaboration to surface was a song, 'Twist The Knife', that appeared on her second album *Furnace Room Lullaby* (2000). And it was no throwaway, British DJ John Peel rating it "one of the best songs in the world, ever". Mike Daly was also involved, along with Case and band member John Ramberg. "It's hard to remember," said Daly when asked about the circumstances surrounding its creation. "It was basically Neko's song – we were hanging out in Seattle on a day off and she came over. Me and Ryan were walking about drinking in the afternoon and then we met up with her, came back to the bus and worked on the song for a while. It was quite an honour – I think it's a great song, but when push comes to shove, it was really her song, we just trimmed the hedges around the yard."

Whiskeytown would release a split single with Neko Case on Bloodshot in 1998. There would be a fringe benefit in this project in that Ryan met Amy Lombardi, PR girl for Neko Case, with whom he'd form a relationship.

Earlier that year, Ryan had made the decision that a change of domestic scenery would be in order. On a whim, he decided to ship all his belongings to Austin, the intention being to rejoin them later when Whiskeytown weren't touring as much. "I just know people too well in Raleigh . . . or not well enough, actually," was his explanation of his move from North Carolina. Being stopped on the street when going to buy a loaf of bread had evidently proved an unnerving experience. Though Whiskeytown's constant touring schedule meant he was rarely at home, one 'home-town' gig in late January was notable in being taped by public broadcast TV for their *Austin City Limits* music show. (A well regarded bootleg has circulated ever since.)

The band continued to tour, embarking on a first ever European visit that kicked off in Stockholm in late April '98. But the fortnight following their last US gig in Atlanta and landfall in Sweden saw the previously hinted-at changes made, Mike Santoro replacing Jenni Snyder on bass "due to lack of . . . ability to play well." Snyder's boyfriend Ed Crawford also bailed out in sympathy at this point, which Ryan considered a "damn shame", though he was happy that less would mean more in musical terms. "We never knew how good we sounded without all those extra members rotting the cheese," he blustered. "Mike has taken over yet another instrument to juggle with on stage (and) Caitlin is very happy as she does not have to tolerate or baby-sit any more – not to mention the guitar (volume) has levelled off enough (for her) to hear her fiddle."

At one of two May gigs at the Borderline, a trendy 250-capacity bar off London's Charing Cross Road beloved of music-biz movers and shakers, Whiskeytown fought against the handicap of playing with unfamiliar rented equipment to entertain the high-powered audience. Judging by the number of people who've since claimed to have been present, this was a landmark gig in terms of introducing Britain to David Ryan Adams (as he had styled himself on the *Strangers Almanac* sleeve).

At the time, his "vibe" was "a cosmic cowboy thing . . . Gram Central", and indeed he was rarely seen out of the Parsons-esque uniform of flared jeans, cowboy boots and cowboy shirts. He and his band had brought to the Borderline an audience primed by an editorial from *Rolling Stone* magazine as the alt.country band with the potential to break out on a scale similar to Nirvana and grunge.

In fact, the Nirvana of which the band was most reminiscent was the *Unplugged In New York* line-up augmented by cellist Lori Goldston.

Melody Maker correspondent Jennifer Nine seemed impressed with what she saw, despite herself. Deeming Adams "nearly as good as he believes he is", she concluded that the band led by "the sullen, black-cloud precocity in a dishevelled suit and messy hair" were miles away from the likes of Golden Smog and Wilco with whom they seemed destined to be bracketed.

But they were not a supergroup in the bracket of The Smashing Pumpkins, who also happened to be in town – so bringing on their guitarist James Iha for the encore was a fairly impressive piece of showmanship. Ryan would repeat the 'star guest' trick nearly four years later at the considerably more spacious Brixton Academy with Oasis' Noel Gallagher, while Iha would soon become a temporary Whiskeytown member as they struggled to commit a final album to tape.

Iha had become hooked on Whiskeytown shortly after hearing an advance copy of *Strangers Almanac*, courtesy of label boss Mark Williams. "Their songs are always instant classics to me," Iha says. "I like their early stuff. The thing is, I never have a problem with any of Ryan's songwriting. He does folk, he does kind of bluesy stuff, he does country, he does rock. And I believe it all. His singing always just sort of puts it across."

Back at the Borderline, Mike Daly certainly appreciated the audience reaction. "People who come to shows (in the UK) are real music fans, and I don't think people in England are quite as over-entertained as people are in the States. Living in New York is like living with constant advertising – every time you open your mailbox there's 44 catalogues – but over in the UK, people don't seem as desensitised. So when they do come to see a show, especially if it's a quieter show, people are really listening. In the States, people will talk in the middle of your set, whereas in England people almost think of it in that kind of movie-theatre setting in a kind of way. And that's great for people performing, it just makes everything better."

Country Music International reader Andrew Coulson of Epsom, who was at one of the shows, called Whiskeytown "quite brilliant" but – controversially in a magazine of this ilk – questioned their right to an 'alt.country' tag. "Anyone who says their appearance at the Borderline was anything but a rock gig must have been at a different show," he opined. "Once stripped of the steel guitar, they are really an extremely talented rock band, albeit with a few minor country influences – a bit like The Eagles before they lost their way." Interestingly, Adams himself had described the intended sound of *Strangers Almanac* as "The Eagles on Quaaludes with a couple of distortion boxes."

Whiskeytown's departure from indie status had led to *Faithless Street* becoming unavailable, leading to the situation where newcoming fans (including, initially, Bob Harris) were under the impression that *Strangers Almanac* was their long-playing début. And that was a situation that made Ryan Adams, for one, uncomfortable. "People are not going to know we have (recorded) stuff that's cooler, less slick, and less intricate," he complained. "I realise that now, but when I made the record, I was making it for myself. We didn't analyse it until later. I actually panicked. 'Oh my God. If this is the first big one, we're fucked. People are going to think we totally *suck.*' "

It was important, therefore, to get *Faithless Street* back on the market. And, happily, a financial arrangement was made between labels past and present to ensure this happened. Its April 1998 reissue on Outpost proved how much Ryan Adams still backed his band's début disc. "I cared about it enough to where I asked Geffen to buy it," he said.

Even long-time fans were persuaded to re-purchase thanks to the inclusion of 11 additional tracks, all recorded with the early Whiskeytown. Three – 'Excuse Me While I Break My Own Heart Tonight', '16 Days', and 'Yesterday's News' – had turned up in 'new and improved' form on *Strangers Almanac*, but the majority was previously unreleased material, some of which came from the *Baseball Park Sessions*. In the reissue's liner notes, Caitlin Cary calls these "songs we maybe didn't appreciate then, but have since come to care about."

The men charged with restoring the grandeur of Whiskeytown's début were Chris Stamey, the individual who'd first hooked them up with Outpost, and much respected engineer Tim Harper, best known for his work with the Connells (of '74–75' hit single fame).

Having been mixed in just two days, *Faithless Street* was a suitable case for a spot of what those in the trade term 'sonic correction and enhancement'. Skillet Gilmore's performances behind the traps had been muddied by improperly triggered bass drum and snare samples. Producers Stamey and Harper not only deleted these in favour of the original drum tracks, but went back to the multi-tracks and rescued vocal, guitar and keyboard licks omitted from the first version. This all improved on the original without detracting from its ramshackle charm.

The band did more than just sit around and watch the restoration process. "We got real particular," said Adams. "It was intense for us to go back and mess with it. We deliberated over the mastering as long as we did to make sure we got it right. It's a precious thing, and I'm really happy with it."

Four takes from the original album's Funny Farm sessions also made their first appearance. 'Lo-Fi Tennessee Mountain Angel' was a live favourite of the time and a song worthy of immortalisation on record, while 'Desperate Ain't Lonely' was a tear-jerking boy/girl duet. The recording of waltz-time 'Tennessee Square' (first sighted on the *Angels* EP) had been unfinished at the close of play, but was considered worthy of completion. Most familiar by far was 'Excuse Me While I Break My Own Heart Tonight', which had appeared on *Strangers Almanac* in re-recorded form while 'Revenge', previously a hidden track, was now officially listed.

Of the *Baseball Park Sessions*, Adams himself has described 'Here's To The Rest Of The World' as "sick good". The alternative title track, 'Empty Baseball Park', was equally impressive, one critic considering it "true to the desolation that has always been the Whiskeytown vision." The song's narrator returns to his home town and runs into an old flame. They wander round looking for something to do.

In comparison with its already released version, '16 Days' was taken at a slightly slower tempo and included some added banjo playing, lending it a more countrified air. The ending was also considerably improved, with Caitlin Cary's violin solo being followed by a guitar solo. This would be one of the rare Whiskeytown songs that would remain in the Ryan Adams set, adding a harmonica to impressive effect.

Adams believed the *Baseball Park* cuts, particularly 'Factory Girl' and 'Here's To The Rest Of The World', were of significance – "the calm before the storm," he called them. "In retrospect, I knew that was the last optimism I was gonna have for a long time. I guess those songs aren't necessarily optimistic, but they definitely aren't as dark as the other stuff."

For Adams, the *Baseball Park Sessions* "show the timeline of learning". They are the missing link between *Faithless Street* and Whiskeytown's later work, and he believed they placed the group's career to the date of re-release (1998) in a much more coherent perspective. "The music is young and naive – and beautiful for it," he says. "There isn't any second-guessing about chords, concepts or styles. It just is what it is, even though the lyrics may be very meditative.

"I think they're that way – more intense, more free-flowing, with more depth – because stylistically we didn't have any preconceptions about what we wanted to do. It was just happening." His conclusion was that, "You can't buy back your naiveté, musically or otherwise – but apparently you can remix and remaster it."

But not everybody believed *Faithless Street*'s new incarnation was superior. "It seems better fed and groomed. It has manners, and the glossy new artwork just doesn't seem to fit with the disc's theme," complained one reviewer. "*Faithless Street* 1995 was lean, its vision unified and desolate. It was scrappy, a survivor despite everything. There's a part of me that really misses that old, ragged disc – poor production and all – that illustrates so eloquently the desperation of the human condition. In the end, though," they concluded, "it's great to get *Faithless Street* back in circulation."

On Whiskeytown's return to native shores from their British trip, they were invited to open for former Creedence Clearwater Revival leader John Fogerty on a two-month summer tour in June 1998, for which they'd warm up with two gigs at the Brewery in Raleigh. It could have been the big break they needed, with crowds of significant size and disposable income ready and willing to be converted to the cause. But the jaunt turned out to be a disaster, the final nail in the coffin of a band whose ability to survive had already been sorely tested.

The Fogerty tour had seen John Wurster replace Skillet Gilmore on drums, Brad Rice (brother of former bassist Jeff) come in on guitar, and Danny Kurtz replace Mike Santoro on bass. Both the latter had played together in The Backsliders, while Rice was a player Adams had long highly regarded. "It's really nice having Brad and Danny in this incarnation of the band," he enthused. "They're older, they're real seasoned musicians (who have) been through it all three times before; they don't put up with any crap. Really, you can say that everybody in the band now has their heads screwed on straight. It's remarkably easy compared to the old days."

The shows took place in front of some of the largest audiences they had played to, filling amphitheatres across the US with the kind of sizeable blue-collar audience Bruce Springsteen was apt to attract. Unfortunately, it was one of Whiskeytown's worst tours ever.

Ryan's bizarre on-stage antics seem to have been enough to drive the headliner's sound engineer to drink. He started turning their sound off as Adams sang his songs backwards, a towel round his head. The singer also took a pop at Fogerty's West Coast roots, a curiosity as Creedence Clearwater Revival had made their name in the late Sixties singing songs about being 'Born On The Bayou'. "Yeah," Ryan declaimed from the stage. "John Fogerty was born on the bayou . . . of Southern California," before closing the show with a provocative cover of Iggy & The Stooges' 'I Wanna Be Your Dog'. (They weren't the first in their field to have adopted that particular anthem, Uncle Tupelo having cut it in 1991 as a potential track for their *Still Feel Gone* album.)

The unlikely pairing of Whiskeytown and Fogerty seems to have lasted through to the beginning of August, when they played Bill Clinton's home town of Little Rock, Arkansas. But in truth Whiskeytown's music hadn't been suited to the less than intimate venues they'd played with Fogerty, let alone the 40-plus age group fan-base who weren't the kind to be impressed by Ryan's habit of lying on his back on stage playing the same note for ten minutes.

Caitlin Cary, as ever, was quick to pour oil on troubled waters. "There's always gonna be dissatisfaction," she stressed post-tour, "and it's just a matter of weighing that in with what's good. I really think that Ryan has a lot of respect for everybody that's in this line-up. He respects us all musically; Brad is one of his guitar heroes from way back and Danny's just solid as can be and really nice. I can see it working out. I don't know if Whiskeytown will last forever, I'm not sure it's that kind of band, but I think that everybody is really committed to the project at hand and we'll just see how it goes after that."

While this tour, of which Ryan claims to have "no memory", was going on, new songs were still being stockpiled. Caitlin had struck up a writing partnership with the ever-present Mike Daly, while Adams had already created much of what would later become *Pneumonia.* Not that the likelihood of a third Whiskeytown album could be taken for granted. Maybe that was a factor in Outpost deciding to re-release *Faithless Street* to a public which for the most part had only heard *Strangers Almanac.*

That was in late September. The eighth of that self-same month had seen Whiskeytown celebrate the occasion with a show at the legendary Fillmore venue in San Francisco where the audience seemed to contain more stars than the stage. Among those in attendance were Jakob Dylan (son of the great Bob, and more recently of Wallflowers fame), Billy Joe Armstrong (Green Day) and actress Winona Ryder, who would crop up again in Ryan's life a couple of years later. The presence of these high-profile onlookers seemed to up the stakes in Adams' eyes, and monitors would be thrown off stage as he became upset about the unsatisfactory sound quality on stage. Indeed, a fight broke out after the set between the singer and the soundman which had to be broken up by Mike Daly.

Postings on the *No Depression* website were highly critical of the evening, but Ryan wasn't going to take that lying down and fiercely fought his corner. "You people suck sometimes," he ranted. "We played a great show. It included some deconstruction at the end, but we played our asses off. And then the little thing at the end . . . for the record, the Fillmore hadn't had rock'n'roll bite it back in the face ever before. I felt like that was a service Whiskeytown could provide. The proverbial biting the hand that feeds idea."

He mocked the suggestion that the venue, which had hosted almost every rock legend of note in its prime, should have been treated with more respect. "The Fillmore isn't any better than some club in your own hometown, only, we're supposed to be honoured. Sorry, no club is lucky enough. We do not discriminate when it comes to manners of what is a good show (*sic*). I'll burn the fucker down next time if they let me. Thanks, and think about the music next time please – all right?"

A typically diplomatic Caitlin was "honoured to get to play at the Fillmore", suggesting the monitor situation may have arisen because the band got there late for their soundcheck. She was again in the situation of having to apologise to people for Ryan, but the Fillmore was implacable and initially withheld the gig fee. Caitlin was hopeful they'd get some money in the end "because I was real nice to everybody afterwards, calmed down the riot and stuff."

Yet the whole scenario inevitably added to the Whiskeytown myth, and even the pragmatic Cary realised that had a value. "Although we will never play the Fillmore and perhaps never get to play in San Francisco again because that guy (the late impresario Bill Graham) owns everything, a lot of people are gonna be talking about that for a long time. Now the question is whether Whiskeytown is a big enough band to be able to get away with that shit. Ryan thinks so." On Ryan's behalf, she denied he had "anger issues or anything like that" and that when he threw a monitor off the stage "he knew full well what he was doing. It's not like (he was) in a blind rage . . . he did not hit anyone."

Unlike the legendary Lansing debacle, the Fillmore show had not been cut short; in fact, Ryan and Caitlin had played an additional mini-set of four or five acoustic songs and Cary didn't think anybody could complain that they hadn't got their money's worth. "They might say that the end was out of hand and stupid but you know, we gave them the goods and then blew up. We've had shows that absolutely sucked and (Ryan) does something stupid and then I feel like we really look dumb, but that was not the case."

After the show, long-suffering tour manager Thomas O'Keefe had asked Adams if there was ever going to be a day when he would be "the regular band guy that goes up and plays a good show every night and there's no antics or crap?" The answer came in almost a whisper: "Yeah, maybe some day." You got the feeling he didn't really believe it himself.

As the autumn tour ended, with tempers strained all round, Whiskeytown looked on the rocks. Ryan had fallen into a deep and passionate relationship with Neko Case's PR girl Amy Lombardi, and seemed set to follow his new love to New York. But the band he'd helped to form wouldn't be cast aside just like that. They had unfinished business binding them together in the shape of an album – *Pneumonia*.

6

A Dose Of Pneumonia

"I ALWAYS FELT like Whiskeytown was like Johnny Thunders and (Lynyrd) Skynyrd and Hüsker Dü and the Mats (Replacements)," Adams told the *St Paul Pioneer Press* of his former band with a definite air of finality. "We just wanted to rock . . . We were called Whiskeytown, and we were from Raleigh. That's part of the problem right there. The hole was dug long before I got my shovel."

And 1999 was the year he would try to put his former band (and many of his former habits) behind him in the most decisive of fashions. Having upped sticks after the doomed '98 tour and swopped Austin for the Big Apple, he had now regained his sanity after the madness of the road. "I don't remember when we went on tour, which clubs we played . . . that's how high I stayed."

There had clearly been a lot going on under the surface. "The tour fizzled out, and if someone wasn't quitting or being fired, they were fucking going to drug rehab or having nervous breakdowns or throwing shit at you on the bus. Or there'd be times when everything would get good and we're all excited and we all wanna win and we're gonna try really hard now. And then the show would fucking suck, or whatever. It just didn't work. It should have showed us."

Relocating to New York to live with Amy Lombardi had, he admitted, been "a heck of a culture shock". The couple leased an apartment on Avenue A between 9th and 10th Streets, and the relationship lit up his very existence. "She changed my whole life," Ryan would later reflect. "I was like one piece of pizza – she taught me how to be the whole pie." With the pressure off, he was happy to hang out in their apartment, pay visits to MOMA (Museum of Modern Art) or the Met (Metropolitan Museum) and look at art. He also got back into his youthful passion, reading. "I tried to finish books. I'd at least start them. I got really interested in a couple of things I've been interested in my whole life but never had the time to dive into, like astronomy and all kinds of cool things." All in all, he summed up, "I had a chance to become a person."

It had clearly given him supreme satisfaction to regain control of his destiny. "It's just a constant struggle to keep the decision-making process on our side of the fence," he explained. "You lose more and more control as your popularity increases, so I fought back . . . I want to take it back in my hands. Because it really got away from me.

"In the band I was probably the most miserable bastard I've ever been in my entire life. For a year. I used to be on stage, dreading it with all of my might. Hating every second of it. And I would just turn it back into the song, make the song good. But I would walk away just dishevelled, upset. I was just kinda like, 'Oh well, whatever. I'm just gonna make little records from now on and it's gonna be fine.' You know, get a job or just go live in the South, 'cause you can live in the South and make little records and have a $500-a-month house and not have to worry about money if you're touring."

His spell in New York would open his eyes to alternative ways of thinking. "Being a Southerner who was always really into the things around me when I've lived in the South, a lot of the things like mysticism, folklore . . . were gone. I don't mean to say that Southerners are full of shit, but *I* definitely was. New York tuned me harder into reality without losing who I was."

Big-city life was initially far from stressful for the country boy. The couple's apartment had a view over Thompson Square Park, while wildlife was present at closer quarters in the shape of a couple of cats (one of which, Lucas, would show up on the inside cover of *Pneumonia*). "My whole life changed," he recalled. "I just wanted to be happy at every moment. And that's really important, because I wasn't that kind of person in my early twenties. I was somebody that was always operating out of fear, I didn't know how to deal with all these adult feelings I had. What I didn't realise was that I had to grow up a little bit, learn some things and open myself up. When you give yourself that kind of time, you get much more in touch with your own spirituality. I did. And I'm happy I did."

New York City was "beautiful and strange and the heat is just this soggy wet blanket of sky getting under my skin a lot" as he, as well no doubt as the other members of Whiskeytown, tried to "go back to our normal lives and experience something called sleep. I am currently in search of a personal life outside of 'twanging effortlessly in an alternative . . . country-rock kinda way'."

Ryan initially revelled in the lack of responsibility only a retired bandleader could appreciate. "I hated being the leader of a band, it just sucked. There's no worse position you could be in." It hadn't taken long, though, before he got a little bored and, in August 1998, decided to start playing music with others again. Newcomer Keith Christopher supplied bass and vocals, while two familiar names, Mike Daly (electric guitar) and Steve Terry (drums) rounded out the line-up. They played at the Mercury Lounge and Coney Island High School that month and, though Ryan dubbed them his "Whiskey-side project" on the *No Depression* bulletin board in order to stir interest, they never officially had a name. "We got lots of sad songs; I thought maybe a few people would want to know," he added somewhat plaintively.

One of Whiskeytown's last acts as a group prior to Ryan's relocation had been to contribute a song for an upcoming Big Star tribute album featuring Juliana Hatfield, Matthew Sweet, R.E.M. bassist Mike Mills, Teenage Fanclub and the Gin Blossoms. At the Ardent Studios in Memphis, Tennessee, Whiskeytown recorded the fan favourite 'Give Me Another Chance', but the album *Big Star, Small World – A Tribute To Alex Chilton* was never released.

And when a tribute album to Gram Parsons was mooted, Ryan was an obvious contender. His version of the track 'A Song For You', originally recorded for the *GP* album, would appear on the summer 2000 various artists release *Return Of The Grievous Angel* (Almo Records). The significant factor here was that he was to be introduced to Emmylou Harris, the singer with whom Parsons had enjoyed a close professional relationship, and this gilt by association was something Ryan revelled in.

It was to prove an experience he would never forget, firstly because Emmy was "one of the only two icons I cared to meet" (Black Flag singer Keith Morris being the other) and also because she proved the key to Gillian Welch and David Rawlings with whom he'd eventually collaborate on his first solo record.

Welch, born in New York and raised in LA, had attended the prestigious Berklee School of Music in Boston, where she and Rawlings had first hooked up. Despite that sophisticated background, it was the simplicity and purity of her work that hit home, having more in common with the Carter Family and Woody Guthrie than current trendsetters. Emmylou Harris' cover of 'Orphan Girl' from her first album *Revival* (1994) had illustrated this, gaining but also losing something in the process. For Ryan Adams, a shark who moved forward yet retained his faith in tradition, Welch and Rawlings would prove perfect partners.

The pair had come up from Nashville and asked Ryan to find them a place in the Big Apple to play. He suggested 11th Street Bar, a drinking establishment just one block away from his own apartment where Celtic music was the order of the day. The Irish folk band playing that night graciously allowed the out of town visitors to do their thing, and Ryan Adams was blown away by what he saw and heard. "Me and Caitlin only had five songs we could do acoustically, but Gill and Dave could sing almost anything the band pulled out. Covers, traditional and their own stuff. I remember leaving that bar and thinking, 'I've got to go to work' . . . I owe them my whole solo career."

But that solo career would have to wait, because the Whiskeytown legacy just wouldn't lie down. Though he'd effectively split the band "because I wasn't home and we weren't rehearsing," they still owed Outpost a further album. "Spiritually the band was over . . . I was just finishing my obligation," was Ryan's way of looking at it. But then again, they had yet to make "a classic album", and, with so much unrecorded material kicking around, it wasn't so surprising he decided one last hurrah was in order.

Accordingly, Adams had agreed to return to the scene of the

'crime' in the spring of 1999 and make another album in upstate New York. But this time it wasn't to be a case of the usual suspects. With Phil Wandscher out of the way, it was effectively now a two-person band – three, if you included Mike Daly.

But anyone who assumed Ryan would now be calling all the shots would have had to reckon with Ethan Johns. The man he'd met during the *Strangers Almanac* sessions would fast become the single most important person in his creative existence. His impact cannot be understated, according to Adams himself. During the *Pneumonia* sessions, Johns pushed his charge in a new direction: for the first time in his musical life, Ryan had discovered that "the harder we worked, the better the record sounded." And taskmaster Johns has to take much of the credit. "I was trying to make this little attitude record," said Adams, "but he had other ideas."

It had been a true triumph for the work ethic. Johns shunned studio trickery, calling his bluff at every stage and encouraging him to rethink his way of working. "Before I met Ethan, I was gonna go in and probably make a record about big C chords and what kind of jeans I was wearing."

As for material, there'd be no problem. The songs, he explained, were "dying to come out". By moving to New York and taking time away from the road, he had "done a bit of growing up . . . Caitlin had also got some clarity on the situation." The absence of former guitar partner Wandscher was, he admitted, "a huge loss" musically, but within the confines of the band the pair had found it impossible to maintain a relationship. "When he wasn't getting my back (up) and babying me I was doing it to him: there's no way that can sustain itself."

Pneumonia was always intended to be Whiskeytown's final will and testament – indeed, the words 'thank you and goodnight' appeared on the penultimate page of the CD booklet – but no one realised when it was recorded that it would take two years to appear, arriving on the racks after Adams' solo début. It was, however, "inevitable this record happened. (I was) trying to take something I'd been taking care of for so long and releasing its potential."

But there would be a definite change of approach, as he told

Billboard.com's Wes Orshoski. "We shot for something grand (and) tried to finally make what all of us felt like a classic record. We dropped a lot of the attitude, and we lost plenty of what is kind of the dumber side of the band, the dumber rock. We just broke it down to trying to play instruments and songs like we'd never done before – with a real sense of community between the different players."

The epic record "obsessed with love and death", was recorded at Dreamland, a converted 19th-century church just outside the town of Woodstock. Not only was Woodstock famous for the 1969 festival that became a blockbuster movie, but it had long been a haunt of artists and musicians, most notably Bob Dylan, The Band and Van Morrison. All these names, of course, have echoed in Ryan's music down the years.

The Whiskeytown band as convened at these sessions revolved around the core duo of Adams on guitar, harmonica, piano and vocals plus Cary on fiddle and duet/background vocals. Mike Daly, as ever, covered a multitude of sins including dulcimer, guitar, keyboards, lap steel guitar, mandocello, mandolin, pedal steel guitar and yet more background vocals.

What remained was mopped up by Richard Causon (keyboards, who would go on to play with Ryan's sometime friend Alanis Morrisette), session player Jennifer Condos (bass, ex-of Don Henley's band) and Whiskeytown road veteran Brad Rice (guitar), while producer and multi-instrumentalist Johns doubled on drums. Most seized upon by the press, though, was the presence of Smashing Pumpkin James Iha (guitar and backing vocals) and ex-Replacement Tommy Stinson (guitar and dobro).

So why had Caitlin Cary endured while so many others had fallen by the wayside? It was a question website interviewer Neal Weiss posed, and her answer then was instructive. "I try every day to get fired and I *can't do it*! I keep asking. Last year we gave Ryan a card for Boss' Day and some nameless person, who has since been fired, wrote, 'Please don't fire me.' I wrote, 'Please fire me,' right underneath it! I stick it out because I can sing with him better than anybody else I've ever found. That's the reason I'm here."

She explained that she respected his talent as a songwriter, "but it's the actual singing that's so great." While she conceded, "He's hard to deal with and he knows it," she explained that rather than being Whiskeytown's mother figure, consoling those at the sharp end of Adams' tongue, she simply kept herself to myself and let the drama develop elsewhere. "Over the years, we've developed a kind of method to deal with each other which is, basically, that I don't deal with any of the bullshit and he doesn't really give it to me much. I hear it for everybody else but it doesn't apply to me."

Sessions for *Pneumonia* were completed in the early summer of '99, just as the Outpost label was becoming enmeshed in a corporate takeover, of which more later. (During the hiatus between recording and release, Adams got into the habit of introducing songs from the sessions when he played them on stage as being from "the album that'll never come out.")

Before going into the studio, Ryan had made some telling comments about the proposed musical direction of the album. "I think people will really freak out how different this next one will be," he told the *Austin Chronicle*. "We want to make a different record every time. We never want to make the same-sounding record . . ." There was no doubt in Caitlin Cary's mind that the magic remained, though her comment suggested this was not quite an authentic group record. "Right now, Whiskeytown is me and Ryan. I love to play and sing with Ryan, and I think he feels the same way."

The album, always slated as a double, would go through the titles *Happy Go Bye Bye* and *Doing That* (a pun on Uncle Tupelo spin-off Wilco's then-popular *Being There*). Johns had been selected as producer over Daniel Lanois, the Canadian who'd worked with U2 and was to help Emmylou Harris fashion her *Wrecking Ball*. Johns had, coincidentally, worked with Harris – an Adams icon – and Linda Ronstadt on their *Western Wall* album produced by his father, Glyn.

Ethan it was who explained the unusual title they ended up with. "The album, lyrically, is about infection, so it's perfect." Ryan went further, likening the recording experience to "the euphoria you get when you're sick. You can see the world from a third-person viewpoint." He also saw his relationship to the band before and after its recording as "a lot like falling into this very slow and sleepy finality: who I was then and who I am now are two very different people. Everything in my life was saying it is time to let go."

So *Pneumonia* was to be a full stop – but a very entertaining one at that. Whether it was Adams' last record with a group or first solo album with some familiar guests, though, is still open to debate. Certainly, the aura it gained while in its two years of limbo has been compared by many to that of Big Star's *Sister Lovers* (also known as *Thirds*) which would not see release until long after Alex Chilton's legendary early-Seventies combo had imploded.

The music kicked off with 'The Ballad Of Carol Lynn', a song whose performance had all the freshness of a first take – the horn section was the only overdub. Ryan wrote the song in 20 minutes while his bandmates were having dinner. Ethan Johns came in, told him to write the bridge and when he returned after supper it was finished. Mike Daly receives the first of seven co-writing credits here, however, suggesting there might have been more to the final arrangement than this instant sketch. Certainly, its funereal pace and piano-led melody is a low-key way to kick off proceedings.

The mandolin-fuelled 'Don't Wanna Know Why' offered a jauntier perspective on life – superficially, anyway. As Adams explained, it was an answer song to "someone I was involved in a scene with" who had penned a song about him called 'You Never Say Goodbye'. "It's one of my rules that I don't say goodbye to people. I don't like it. I would be at a party and, instead of explaining why I was going to split, I'd go." This Fleetwood Mac-inflected number was his attempt to redress the balance.

The song written about him "wasn't harsh", and neither was his response. "I tried to think about . . . what I had invested in the whole situation and my analysis was . . . nothing." He concluded that, "It's either me making fun of myself or being so non-committal or it's me saying it would be impossible for anyone . . . to have any real true feelings about me when I am ever so changing."

The solo-penned 'Jacksonville Skyline' has an immediate parallel in the title to Dylan's *Nashville Skyline* album, but owed more to Steve Earle's small-town tales. It told of Adams' youth with a weeping steel guitar backdrop and was strewn with images so clear, one reviewer noted, "you could be staring at the work of a pavement artist". This was followed by the even more low-key 'Reason To Lie', co-penned with Mike Daly with a violin refrain from Cary not unlike Rod Stewart's early solo work. This happily distracted from the lyric, which wasn't Adams' best.

'Don't Be Sad', track five and the first single from the album, was paradoxically the first departure from the typical 'Whiskeytown sound'. "Thank God," quoth its singer, "because what does *that* mean anyway?" Ironically, he suggested, "we may have found our voice when we went hoarse." Guesting Pumpkin James Iha picked up his sole co-writing credit here, and it was undoubtedly his sparkling intro guitar figure over what was an almost funky drum track that caught the ear. British Eighties hopefuls Prefab Sprout almost came to mind for their "breezy wistfulness".

On a lyrical level, Adams was sending a mixed message to "someone I really cared about". On the one hand, he was telling them to "hang in there . . . we're going to make it" but at the same time saying "there's no way in hell it's going to happen." The song was one he'd later refuse to listen to because it foretold events that actually happened. "It scares the shit out of me," he cheerfully confessed. Yet there were some who would single this out as *Pneumonia*'s key track: a 'zeitgeist-defining' song akin to 'Bittersweet Symphony' (The Verve), 'Wonderwall' (Oasis) or 'A Design For Life' (Manic Street Preachers).

'Sit And Listen To The Rain' was an Adams take on Bruce Springsteen's small-town angst – but instead of going down to the river, he sat inside and, reflecting his Jacksonville past, hoping for decent re-runs (repeats) on the television. "I'll never understand this emptiness," he moaned over a strummy, almost Smiths-ian backing – not one of the album highlights and a late addition to the running order that didn't feature on the 'pre-release' version.

The very solo 'Under Your Breath' was acclaimed as revealing "complex emotional turmoil" – yet Mike Daly, who shared the credit with Ryan, has since claimed authorship of a title bearing both names as writers. "That's one song I wrote that I really feel like I had nothing to do with. It just kind of came through me; I was just happy to be the antenna that picked it up. Alan (Edwards, singer of the Charlotteville, NC, band Lou Ford) is a good friend of mine. His band was playing in New York and he stayed at my place – and I got up before him the next morning and started writing the song in probably about an hour – Alan came in and he was all hung-over and he went, 'Man, that song's *really* good.' And I said, 'Thanks', and he was like, 'No, that song's really *really* good.' I am proud of it. It's definitely a song that people can identify with, and that's what it's all about – making a connection."

Next up, the very McCartney-esque 'Mirror Mirror' boasted lyrics that were written by Ryan at the Woodstock Inn in the early morning, the music being completed the next day. Wired and unable to sleep after a hard day in the studio, Adams and crew called up the bar and drove there "in incredible amounts of snow" to sit by the fire and enjoy an "amazing" jukebox. Ryan, who "had this moment", asked the bartender for a napkin and wrote the words down in one sitting. The pop song that leapt out once in the studio would not have been out of place on *Sgt. Pepper* – indeed, several reviews pointed to a similarity. Not a song for Whiskeytown's past fans, but a possible pointer to a more commercial future.

The horns and woodwinds overdubbed on this jaunty cut gave it a real late-Sixties Beatles feel – as far from typical Whiskeytown as we'd heard. "It was more voiced than Whiskeytown should sound like," he'd later reflect, "because Caitlin loved the melody so much." Certainly, her backing vocals added an optimistic note to proceedings – no bad thing in the context of the album. Yet the lyric of 'Mirror Mirror' was, according to Adams, no throwaway matter. "(This was) one of the songs when I took a cold hard look at myself. About who I was, what was happening."

The almost tropical style of 'Paper Moon' threw in yet another change of pace, and would have little to commend it to fans of Whiskeytown's signature 'ragged but right' sound. With tuned percussion twinkling in the background, a mandolin solo added to the unworldliness of the track. Things got even more surreal later on with a slurpy string arrangement recorded by Ethan Johns' father Glyn. Lyrics? "I'm her baby doll, she's my cup of tea . . ." Some reviewers quoted Cole Porter as a reference point, something surely even Ryan couldn't have contemplated. Certainly, it was a style not heard from him before.

The album jolted back on track with 'What The Devil Wanted' – like 'Mirror Mirror' a softly spoken and seemingly autobiographical song. Sung over Mike Daly's solo keyboard, it conjured up an almost Nick Drake-like ambience. As its title suggests, 'Crazy About You' was a conventional (by Adams standards) love song suspended above some vaguely Rolling Stones-y chords and could, as one critic suggested, have been the vehicle for "some Nashville lass to ride to the top of the country charts."

'Back down in My Hometown everybody's feeling it bad,' Ryan advised in the album's downbeat twelfth cut, allowing Jacksonville a taste of the spotlight. He also alluded to his current life in New York State, with money running out but his honey keeping him safe and sound.

'Easy Hearts', "a pretty heavy song" according to Ryan, was cut completely live with nine people singing and playing together. Carried away with the spiritual experience of singing in the belfry of a church, Adams lifted his head up and sang at the top of his lungs, no longer using the microphone in front of his face. The result leaked into every other live microphone in the room, but fortunately there were no mistakes.

The song was important to its writer because it was a plea from a penitent young man, "this person saying, 'At the end of my screwing up, when I am maybe completely destitute, crushed, can I crawl to your doorstep and will you let me in?' There was a time that was happening for more than one person in the band, when we knew we were about to reach a peak of self abuse. I know who I was writing the song about and she knows who I was writing about. We both peaked and hit bottom at the same time."

'Bar Lights' ended the album with what Ethan Johns (who chose it as the closer) called "an honest moment". He'd always faded the performance on previous rough mixes, but when he listened again to the way the take fell apart (for the first time since the track was cut) he considered it a highly appropriate way to bring proceedings – and Whiskeytown's career – to a close.

He admits he'd had his mind on something else when he heard Ryan announce, "Let's go to the bar," as the music in the studio speakers ended. But the effect, Johns insisted, was symbolic. "He'd given me his take and that was it, you're losing me now. And that was perfect, 'cos it's so Ryan. I've just given you a gift, now I'm taking time for myself."

In a manner reminiscent of The Pogues with Kirsty MacColl, Adams and Cary gave the song their best Parsons/Harris duet vocal over an upbeat tempo laced with violin and mandolin. With the lights reflecting on the bottles and in the glasses, Ryan has five more dollars in his pocket and is writing his number on a matchbook sleeve. Typical of Adams' life revolving round licensed premises – even the music publishing credit read 'Barland Music'!

As Ryan dissolved into laughter, he explained as the backing continued: "I broke a string right after that happened. I forgot a line, started laughing and then a string broke. All right, I'm going to the bar. Fuck *this* . . ."

But in spite of the impression this parting shot gave, that wasn't to be all there was. The hidden fifteenth song, 'To Be Evil' was not only the last song to be cut but "a track that *had* to be on the record . . . it's important to me. It was a really good look at some of the shitty things I do, people do, when they're confused and not sure of themselves.

"It helps me to know that it's on there because it was my . . . goodbye to all this years in Whiskeytown and all those things . . . sometimes horror, sometimes beauty. It was important for that to be the last thing, to say: 'Hey, I never meant to hurt anybody and I never meant anybody to get damaged or confused.' But in your youth you're scared, you don't know how to deal (with it)."

After the album had been mixed in Los Angeles, there came a re-run of the *Baseball Park Sessions* incident when the record company ordered them back to the studio for a re-mix by Scott Litt, one third of the Outpost founding triumvirate whose previous charges had included Nirvana and R.E.M. He "cleaned its face" in a way the band didn't approve of, but Ethan Johns and Ryan would eventually reclaim the master tapes in late 2000 and remix a single album's worth of music, vowing to give the result a "vintage

Stones/Beatles sound" that redefined *Pneumonia* as a more logical bridge between the all-out country-rock of *Strangers Almanac* to the relative refinement of solo début *Heartbreaker.*

Not that returning to Whiskeytown yet again would prove a pleasant experience for Adams. "There were times in the mixing room that were absolutely heavy for me, moments when I was revisiting a place I didn't want to be back in at all but I had to deal with and it drove me a bit crazy."

Label boss Mark Williams pointed out that the delay in release gave Johns and Adams an opportunity that most artists and producers never get – the chance to live with a record for more than a year after completion and revise it. People were divided as to whether this was a plus or a minus, as Johns' and Adams' remix was considered to have lost some of the warmth of the 'Napster version'.

Whatever the truth, the new *Pneumonia* featured a radically different track listing, lacking original inclusions 'Choked Up' and 'Tilt-a-Whirl'. Both the omitted songs would show up on the bootleg *Silver And Gold Volume 2*, the former a strummed acoustic love song with a catchy, repetitive piano figure, the latter a more mellow, downbeat affair. (A band called Minibar, about which little is known, also covered 'Choked Up', and their version would appear on the 2001 soundtrack to teen movie *Jay & Silent Bob Strike Back.*)

But Adams, as "the one that went and saved it and released it," believed he and he alone should be the judge of what the record was. "The *Pneumonia* that is so lauded is the original that people heard on-line, but that was not our version, it was the record label's. Our label at the time, the Geffen people, took together a bunch of different clips from different sessions that were not supposed to be a part of it and stuck them together.

"I think that was kind of a crap thing, because *Pneumonia*, all its glory and beauty, was really what we did in that church. Anybody that thinks any differently . . . (When) people in our hometown go, 'The original's better!', I just look at them, and I go: 'Well, you'd think *I'd* fucking know what the original was, considering I was the guy that wrote the fucking *songs*!' "

Reviews of the album were unanimously upbeat, and there's little doubt that the general level of interest was raised by it following in the footsteps of *Heartbreaker. Classic Rock* magazine's Phil Wilding, a long-time fan, even closed his eyes and ears to Adams' solo début, considering *Pneumonia* to continue *Strangers Almanac*'s "slow descent into despair. What a self-doubting, magically run-down romantic Ryan is. Gram Parsons is dead and Paul Westerberg doesn't seem to want to work much anymore, which leaves Ryan as the last chronicler of Middle America's bar land."

In general, 70 per cent of the reviews believed that *Pneumonia* had been worth the wait, the remaining 30 per cent feeling it hadn't quite lived up to the hype. And even those not totally sold on it could come up with a quotable line: how about, "If you've been waiting for the next Bob Dylan, forget it, but inside Adams' heart is as good a place as any to rest awhile."?

Even *No Depression* magazine, whom one might have expected to have lost some patience with their former favourite, still kept the faith. "Some may feel *Pneumonia* lacks the emotional weight of *Heartbreaker*," said their Erik Flannigan, "but beneath all of these gorgeous performances, Ryan Adams just may be revealing himself. The last words he sings . . . are, 'I'm not evil, I'm just scared.' I believe him. And even if he's only fooling us, he's doing one hell of a job."

Adams confirmed he had "spiritually checked out" of Whiskeytown but nevertheless had planned to reunite with his friends for a New York show to deliver what he described as a "perfect presentation of *Pneumonia*."

Indeed, Adams, Cary and Daly would play a number of post-recording shows with a revolving-door cast of guitarists, bassists, and drummers. Daly felt the recording sessions had been "such a great process. Outpost was excited, and we were excited. And then everything just ground to a halt. It was so hard to work on something so passionately and then have this happen."

'This' was the merger between Universal and Polygram in 1999 that rocked not only Whiskeytown but the music business in general. The Geffen and A&M labels were folded into Interscope, and Whiskeytown's label, Outpost, was left out in the cold – the unwanted acquisition. Certain acts, like Crystal Method and Days Of The New, would simply transfer to Interscope, but Mark Williams feared that Whiskeytown's album would get lost in the shuffle and wanted to find a more suitable home for it.

Adams was understandably unhappy with the situation, and told the *New York Times* so: "Basically the guy (Edgar Bronfman) who owns Seagrams and a couple of other companies – this man, he has a son. He probably asked his son what businesses he wanted to run, and he said he wanted to run the music business. So he bought his son Universal. Disgusting, really. So he bought it, and got rid of anybody that didn't sell a million copies the last couple of records."

The impasse would have a damaging effect on Ryan Adams' finances. So broke was he, in fact, as he waited in vain for *Pneumonia* to emerge that he approached guitar shops for jobs, while the Bottom Line Club in Greenwich Village turned down his application to be their soundman.

But he was far from down and out. While enjoying domestic bliss in New York City, he'd found himself writing songs again. Once that happened, it was somehow inevitable that he'd eventually begin playing shows. He tested the water in New York's Mercury Lounge in August 1999 before heading back to home turf. A date at Chapel Hill's Local 506 found Caitlin Cary in the house and happy to guest on a slower, more heartfelt version of 'Inn Town' ("I'll always want to play with him," she said, "and there's no doubt in my mind that he'll always want to play with me"), while moral support for a two-nighter at the Brewery in Raleigh was supplied by Chip Robinson and Kenny Roby.

They played under the name of Battlestar Connecticut and included in their set four songs written especially for the night during the soundcheck. A poster on the Whiskeytown-avenues mailing list, one Jay Holden, rated it "the loudest event I've ever been a part of – a rock band with Chip Robinson on bass, Ryan guitar and vox and another guitar and drummer . . . can't remember their names."

Everything still functioned according to expectations, one assumes, because shortly afterwards, armed with a notebook of new songs (most of which remain unreleased), Adams set out on a short tour of the South-east US. Kicking off in Athens, Georgia (the home of R.E.M.) at the 40 Watt, he called in at Chattanooga, Tennessee, Atlanta, and Birmingham, Alabama before landing up in Nashville. There, at the Exit/In, he played alongside Gillian Welch before returning to his home state of North Carolina to wrap things up at Asheville's Almost Blue club.

Returning to New York City, he played a pseudonymous pre-Christmas gig at the Continental as Snow Kobra (the name of a band he'd reportedly started with Jesse Malin of D Generation) before settling down for the season.

The bug had clearly not left him, though, and when the highly rated Marah cancelled an engagement at the Mercury Lounge in early January 2000 he needed little persuasion to rearrange his evening. That last-minute decision was music to the ears of a bunch of former Whiskeytown fans who'd heard about the gig by word of mouth. Appropriately, Mike Daly – "the Sideshow Bob of Whiskeytown", as he was introduced – was present to help him out on *Strangers Almanac* highlights 'Houses On The Hill', '16 Days' and 'Dancing With The Women At The Bar'.

The remaining 13 songs performed in the two-hour comeback set would not have been as familiar, however. Nor were they to their writer, who regularly checked his lyrics from a notebook. Among them were 'Born Yesterday' and 'The Poison And The Pain', neither of which would make it to his next release. The on-stage jokes and wit contrasted with the downbeat nature of nearly all the songs – so much so that he developed the running joke of introducing each of them as "another sad song about . . . me". Yet the response he received could have left him in little doubt that he could spend his evenings more profitably than slumped in a chair watching TV movies.

It would take until May 2001 for the album recorded in Woodstock in 1999 to see the light of day, adding to the air of mystery surrounding it. "When it does finally come out," Ryan emphasised, "there's no band to tour because there isn't a Whiskeytown any more. But we'll all sort of be sitting back in our collective lives with a big grin on our faces."

Mike Daly hoped the band's albums would not only be enjoyed

for years but also discovered by new generations. "I'm proud of what the band stood for, which I think was like all the bands that we grew up on, their kind of ethics. It was everything I loved about The Stones and The Beatles. It was everything that Ryan loved about Black Flag. It was everything that Caitlin loved about Dusty Springfield . . . I think Whiskeytown will be like that beautiful diamond in the rough that you would never want to polish any further. You'd just want to let it be."

No matter how *Pneumonia* might have been billed, Whiskeytown fans would still live in the hope that their "whole lot of back catalogue stuff" might one day see the light. "I'd rather let that lie where it is for a long time," said Adams, "because I don't really care to listen through it. I'm still writing; I'm still working forward. Somebody else can go and do that. Maybe Caitlin or Mike Daly could assemble that stuff." For Ryan Adams, the future was bright: the future was solo.

So, sadly, was the state of his personal life too, as his relationship with Amy drew to a close. It had, it seems, been on the cards for some while. That final 1999–2000 winter in New York saw Ryan sick with flu in unfriendly sub-zero temperatures almost all the time. And when the relationship foundered it left him "so distraught" that even The Smiths, whose *Meat Is Murder* made a return to his turntable, proved inadequate solace. That joke certainly wasn't funny anymore, so he decided on a drastic course of action – to turn his back on the Big Apple and return down South where he could skateboard again, feel the sun on his back and get back to his old ways.

He returned to North Carolina with a broken heart but a renewed artistic will. "I'd had enough of New York," Adams reflects. "My lease was running out, I had a relationship on the rocks, I was having some record company problems, I'd taken some serious blows that year, and I just needed to escape. I was afraid, but I knew if I gave in to any of that fear I would just crumble into pieces."

He met Frank Callari, a music business veteran who had worked with such varied artists as British industrial rockers New Order and US Alice Cooper clone Marilyn Manson. More relevantly to Ryan, he already looked after the careers of up-and-coming alt.country acts The Mavericks (who'd made the crossover to mainstream) and Lucinda Williams (who was on the cusp). He was already a fan of Whiskeytown, so he was interested when he heard their singer was looking for a manager.

He was wary, however, having heard horror stories about Adams' rebellious behaviour and only agreed to accept him on a probational basis: "He wanted to see if I was gonna fall apart," admitted Ryan. Callari felt his new charge "was just overwhelmed by all the attention he started getting at 21 and was just doing what he thought a rock'n'roll rebel was supposed to do . . . probably drinking and druggin' too much." Such 'fun' ran the risk of ruining his career, so the deal would go through only "if he wanted to straighten out and get focused about his career, if he was ready to get serious."

It only took a week for Ryan to decide he was ready.

7

Profit From Heartbreak

"WRITING FOR A band, you can't be as self-evocative and forthcoming, because then it just looks sort of contrived – to me, anyway. When I make solo records, I think I'm able to explore more . . . so it's like telling a story about myself, or my reflections, and less about the force of the band. Because great rock'n'roll bands are about attitude and believability – you just go forward with things and let them live with that format. But a solo record is really about me trying to exhume things in myself that I wasn't aware of."

Relationships often happen on the rebound. Ryan Adams quit New York after well over a year living there and, two weeks after landing in his chosen base of Nashville in the summer of 2000, turned in *Heartbreaker*. His relationship with Music City would be a love/hate one over the years, but for the moment love was winning out. He described his new home as a "boot camp for music. I went there and got my mind blown by people who made me feel like I had been a lazy fuck for a long time," he said. "I had stuff to learn."

His major aim in life now was "just trying to be a person, and let go of a lot of stuff. Sometimes you make records to further your career. I didn't think I had a career to further." As soon as he'd emotionally 'let go' of *Pneumonia*, he found himself writing "self-sufficient songs on acoustic guitar and trying to understand folk music and gospel music."

The new solo star would hit the ground running almost as soon as he arrived. And he was indebted to his friends Welch and Rawlings for making it easy. "The record," he'd explain, "got written hanging out at Gillian and Dave's house, or at my house, or a couple of them in the Studios, five minutes from my house." Spontaneity was the key – the slurring tape noise at the beginning of 'Damn, Sam (I Love A Woman That Rains)' is Ethan Johns rushing to press the record button – and the whole thing would be finished after just 14 days.

"I went to Nashville for professional and romantic rehabilitation," Ryan revealed. "I just had to get out of New York, I'd been in the city for too long. It's no mystery, because of the way *Heartbreaker* sounds: I left a relationship, I left a lot of things behind. It just was I kind of needed to get out, and I needed to get away from everything. So I split." *En route*, he played half a dozen gigs on the West Coast with Kim Richey and a handful solo in Austin to keep ring-rust at bay.

He'd brought one or two songs with him to start things off. 'Oh My Sweet Carolina' had emerged near the end of his New York stay, while 'My Winding Wheel' came to him while riding in the self-drive truck taking his possessions to his new home at an East Nashville address. Adams was playing guitar in the passenger seat, and clearly spinning such a spell over his friend the driver that a crash all but ensued: indeed, he credits the fingering of a suspended chord in the song to the fact that he flinched, anticipating the inevitable collision.

The collision between Adams and Music City would be an interesting one, too. His spell there was about "trying to understand some of the processes I was getting used to from all the people I was around," he said, summing up the time as "a creative exile".

He saw two different tribes at work – 'honkies' who "go to work or do other Music Row shit . . . get off work at five and they go out between six and nine. Then around nine or ten o'clock the underbelly comes out. Like Billy Mercer and me and Lucinda Williams . . . We're playing shows at like 11 o'clock or whatever. So the kids rule the night-time." For this reason, he wouldn't go out to eat until after 9 o'clock to avoid "a bunch of fuckin' loser white people who don't know anything . . . Honkies. I can't stand 'em."

He reserved equal venom for the commercially successful 'new country' stars who'd revitalised the music's commercial standing, likening them to heavy metal outfit Def Leppard (though curiously professing to like Shania Twain, wife of long-time Leppard producer 'Mutt' Lange). These acts had all modelled themselves on The Eagles, he ranted, "and The Eagles were way better than *any* of that stuff."

He reserved particular scorn for 'hat acts' like Travis Tritt and Kenny Chesney, singer of 'She Thinks My Tractor's Sexy'. "You can just see people sitting around in Nashville offices coming up with song titles like that. I remember hearing that and going, 'Y'know, I'm from North Carolina and as far as I'm concerned when I think about the South I think about William Faulkner or Howard Feinster's artwork.' If that guy was standing next to me and started singing that tractor song, I literally would have punched him in his face. I'd be like, 'How dare you undermine a complete working class?!' But the thing is, nobody takes that shit seriously, it's like watching a cartoon."

All these comments would have sounded hollow had not Adams' music backed up his right to be taken seriously as a solo artist. And it was his partnership with Ethan Johns, ignited during the recording of *Pneumonia*, that would keep him on track to deliver. Fascinatingly, Ethan's father Glyn Johns had endured a similar battle with The Eagles when producing their first two albums back in the early Seventies, banishing them to the studio toilets if they required so much as a puff of marijuana.

Johns Junior had already informed Ryan that drinking in the studio would not be tolerated, regarding it as "such a minor part of what's going on creatively." Johns believed Adams had lacked focus, and that his gift for pulling out a spellbinding take was often masked by drink. Surprisingly, perhaps, this met with a positive response from the artist. Having initially told Johns he would never know the difference whether he was drunk or sober, he put up his hands. "I slowed the car down, put it at the side of the road and got a taxi."

He'd also changed his tipple of choice from 'brown liquors' such as bourbon to vodka, apparently on the advice of Keith Richards. "I must have had a hangover for two years," he reflected. "But you have to go out of your way to get hammered on vodka.

You don't start slurring, and playing with handguns doesn't become a good idea at one in the morning. I never liked that feeling." He was now "trying to ease off the heaviness of things . . . trying to enjoy stuff. I think I've reached a point where I kind of know how to take care of myself, keep those situations and feelings at bay."

The initial results could be seen in the songwriting. Living the bar-room life, as Ryan did, was all very well for collecting stories but he'd "get loaded" and, at two in the morning, "half write what could have been a great song – or maybe I just wasn't thinking it through." That's how he had made records in his previous life – indeed, a lot of great records are made that way – but now, "instead of collecting little snippets from my very dark, secluded world, I came out the other end (as) someone who could hum a tune I never heard before while walking the street and turn it into a song by the time I get to the studio.

"I was always playing music but never respecting the process," he concluded. The process in the case of *Heartbreaker* would be as straightforward as you like. Cut in Room A of Woodland Studios, a four-piece band of Adams, Rawlings, Welch and Johns laid down the basic tracks, with occasional help from Pat Sansone, a talented keyboardist/multi-instrumentalist who had played with Amy Rigby, the Squirrel Nut Zippers, the Autumn Defense and others. There was also a trio of guest vocalists, of whom more later. Adams' solo début would come together in the space of just 11 hard-working days.

The future of Woodland Studios at Five Points in East Nashville, built as a theatre in 1920, had been in jeopardy since its structure had suffered extensive tornado damage. In 1964, the building had been transformed into one of Nashville's first and best recording studios where such veterans as Merle Haggard and Neil Young recorded, but since the twisters had wreaked their havoc the studio had sat empty, and for sale, for more than a year.

The new, sober writing regime that had yielded an album's worth of songs in record time seemed to be working, all kinds of new influences unfurling onto a blank canvas. "I was rolling through a lot of different progressions and styles and just didn't stop myself," he told the *Guardian*'s Adam Sweeting. He also explained he believed his lack of conventional instrumental ability had served him well in the writing of songs. "I'm not really qualified to sit and learn new guitar licks or piano licks. For me, writing a song's down to how I play an instrument. It's like open verse to me. It's how I enjoy myself musically."

The packaging portrayed Ryan as a bedsit balladeer, enjoying a solitary cigarette (in a reclining position) on the cover shot plus a series of contemplative blue-washed pictures on the fold-out. Only a picture of him flanked by Gillian and David broke the mood, a totally unrelated shot of Ryan at a convenience store checkout completing the package.

Many albums have signalled their intention to be different by starting off with a little informal studio chat. But 'Heartbreaker' trumps even these by giving the spoken lead-in both a title ('Argument With David Rawlings Concerning Morrissey') and a track one label. As they eventually conclude, the difference of opinion as to whether the song 'Suedehead' appears on *Viva Hate* or *Bona Drag* is irrelevant, as it is on both records.

Ryan liked the contrast. "It's absolutely off-the-cuff, and the reason we left it is because we thought it was absolutely hilarious . . . I mean, we were just totally fucking with each other. The main reason I think that we left it in was firstly because every time we ever hear it, all of us just die laughing, and secondly that conversation is going on and then 'To Be Young . . .' comes in and the contrast is excruciating. The track comes out of the barrel like a fuckin' bullet out of a gun."

Disregarding the unwieldy title, 'To Be Young (Is To Be Sad, Is To Be High)' is a Wilbury-esque take on Bob Dylan from a Tom Petty standpoint. It was the first of three tracks to feature a shared credit, co-written as it was with Dave Rawlings who contributed outstanding lead guitar to the recorded version. Adams' vocals are out front and focused in a way they never were with Whiskeytown – and though the loss of Caitlin's sure harmony was felt for a brief minute, the momentum here carried proceedings. It was clear this was a new ball game.

'To Be Young' was made to be a concert standout and was

first performed solo in February 2000, the month it was written. But its easy-rocking vibe also made it a candidate for band performance.

'My Winding Wheel' would also become a concert classic, made for audience participation, and has been played at almost every show Adams has given since 2000. It's a song in which he complains he feels like a map "without a single place to go", but the organ, acoustic guitar and drums propulsion means the song sounds anything but directionless. It's tended to be performed slower and more bluesily of late.

As you'd expect, the song entitled 'AMY' was as personal as anything on the album, but the slightly cloying orchestral arrangement and vocal harmonies owe more to Crosby Stills & Nash. (Interestingly, he'd take to performing CSN&Y's 'Helpless' live, sometimes straight with Welch on harmonies and other times with a spoof lyric, retitling it 'Laundry'.) The opening line of his own song, "I don't know why I let go," set the tone for a somewhat banal lyric by Adams' high standards.

This would be the only track title on the album rendered in capitals "because I was finally making a huge statement about somebody that a lot of my songs and a lot of my life had been about for a long time . . . I was going to write something I really *needed* to." Cathartic it may have been, but if the intention was a reconciliation, it didn't work. "She's heard it, obviously," he'd later reveal. "But it didn't do anything for us . . . she and I are just too poisonous to one another."

Indeed, there'd be an unwelcome sequel to this when Lombardi's last name and place of work was printed in a magazine. She became the target of crank calls and had to quit her job. It was Ryan's first experience of a "fucked up" press; little wonder the pair were no longer on speaking terms. Possibly for this reason, the song was rarely performed live after the end of 2000, though its return to the set list in early 2002 suggested a possible *rapprochement*.

A classic 'on the road' song, 'Oh My Sweet Carolina' would be special even without the stupendous harmony vocal of Emmylou Harris which chimed in on the chorus. It's also the track where Pat Sansone's piano made its biggest impression, rolling through the mid section and winning the accolade from *Modern Rock* magazine: "Sansone contributes a nice honky-tonk piano solo to what is one of the best songs of Adams' relatively brief career." Imagery like, 'The sunset's just my light bulb burnin' out' makes this a moving few minutes indeed.

Adams and Harris had encountered each other on the *Return Of The Grievous Angel* project, the tribute album of Gram Parsons covers to which Ryan had contributed and which was released in the summer of 1999 – and this was the payback. At that point, he'd explain, "She wasn't like a real person to me, she was an icon to me. I'd put a lot of time into listening to her, and Gram as well. I'd almost studied their records." Maybe too much: the *Austin Chronicle* reckoned his take on his hero's 'A Song For You' was "faithful to the point of redundancy."

The introduction had, as ever, been made by Ethan Johns, and led to a duet on live television. The song in that instance was 'Return Of The Grievous Angel', and Ryan was "scared out of my mind that I was gonna fuck it up. But what really freaked Emmy out was me going to see her at the Ryman Auditorium in Nashville, and I'd just had a birthday. Her mother asked me when my birthday was, and I said, 'November 5.' And she said, 'You know . . .' And I said, 'I know' . . ."

'Bartering Lines' is the first of two songs on the album co-written with Van Alston, credited as 'Renaissance Man of Raleigh, North Carolina'. Alston was Ryan's tour manager, co-owner of the Lakewood Lounge club in Raleigh and owner of Ricebox Records – "an all-round great guy". The pair apparently collaborated on a potential second Adams solo effort titled 'Four Track Mind', demos for which were recorded in Van's kitchen.

More noticeable on the recording was Gillian Welch's keening harmonies over a stark Neil Young-style banjo backing. Pat Sansone contributed what the sleeve called a "weird stomp-producing organ-type instrument", adding to the growing intensity of the moment. Perhaps due to this, it was a song that was very rarely essayed live, though the end of 2001 saw a band version, still acoustic, worked up. The concept of comparing love to money saved and spent was unusual and effective.

Having kept the quality up for five consecutive songs, *Heartbreaker* now let its guard slip somewhat. 'Call Me On Your Way Back Home', unadorned guitar and voice for the first half of its performance, was the first let-up in the album's excellence, slipping by relatively unnoticed due to the lack of an identifiable chorus or melody. (To be fair, his live version held more conviction.) 'Damn, Sam (I Love A Woman That Rains)' was another lesser song – very brief too at just two minutes and eight seconds. But as the album continued, it was apparent this less than distinguished brace was to give the listener a breather.

The provocative lyric of 'Come Pick Me Up', relating to a highly dysfunctional relationship, would always make it one of the album's more controversial tracks. This was the second Van Alston co-write, and was created backstage at the second of two dates played at the Tractor Tavern in Seattle in February 2000. Played live that night, it's been loudly requested (and played) at almost every Adams gig since. That first live performance of this song featured tour-mate Kim Richey as his vocal foil on the chorus, a role she would happily reprise in the studio (though the lyrics changed substantially in the meanwhile), while the unashamedly Dylan-esque puff-and-suck harmonica added salty punctuation.

Adams delivered the following explanation of his inspiration from the stage in 2001. "Some people think this song is autobiographical, but it's not. It's about like walking into a bar and you see this girl and she's so fucking hot . . . but it's like sometimes, before you head over and talk to her, you start thinking like, 'I just *know* you're going to totally fuck me off, fuck all of my shit up, throw a rock through my window, take my records . . . but it's absolutely worth it, just take me home now . . . So there really are adversaries in the song . . . because the girl screws the guy over and the guy gets screwed in more ways than one."

Into double figures on the track counter with 'To Be The One', and there's more harmonica but considerably less instrumentation. This really *is* Bob Dylan circa '64, it seems at first, but it just dwindles. Another female vocalist, Allison Pierce, makes a contribution to 'Why Do They Leave?', which has a slow-paced country-soul vibe straight out of Muscle Shoals that adds to the allure. Again, though, not a song that would be regularly mentioned in dispatches.

Anyone expecting a Springsteen-esque blowout from the title 'Shakedown On 9th Street' might have been surprised to hear a rockabilly-styled retro-gallop reminiscent of Dwight Twilley or maybe John Hiatt at his rowdiest. The lyric referred to a street brawl that saw Ryan's girl, Lucy, hurt and the song as a whole would become something of a live standard, offering considerable scope for instrumental jamming. Like 'To Be Young', it lifts the mood at a crucial point in proceedings.

'Don't Ask For The Water' is very, very much in Bob Dylan misogynist mode. The line that first follows the title, 'She'll swallow you down', tells the story. This is a story of being used and abused by a former lover, the backing of acoustic guitar and (eventually harmonica) adding melancholy. "Tired and tender" was one critic's view.

'In My Time Of Need' finds Adams sounding genuinely weary, as if he's poured his heart out one time too often. Minimal backing includes Gillian Welch's sparing harmony and the muted plucking of a banjo, giving this a resonance that would have seen it fit nicely on Neil Young's *On The Beach*. Rumour has it the song was set to be covered by Johnny Cash, but the Man in Black's continuing ill health caused the session to be cancelled at the last minute.

The song had quite a history, having originally been written during the sessions for *Pneumonia* and recorded by Whiskeytown as a simple acoustic guitar and percussion piece. (This version appears on the bootleg *Pneumonia Demos*.) When he's performed the song, Adams has said the song was inspired by a guy who used to hang around the studio and didn't say much. This was his attempt to get inside his head.

But the last word was reserved for 'Sweet Lil Gal (23rd/1st)', a lurching piano ballad heavy on the bass keys until the late-song intrusion of a guitar. It's a song that serves the purpose of ending the album but is probably not one of Adams' greatest. When performed live, it was usually played with acoustic guitar backing, suggesting Ryan himself was uncertain about it. The girl in question hangs round the cigarette machine and when you're lonely 'makes you feel nice'.

Country Music International hailed *Heartbreaker* as "a lo-fi country-rock record with an experimental edge," though they felt Adams "doesn't possess that magic, intangible ingredient that made Gram Parsons a legendary musical leader. He is a follower rather than an innovator."

Bob Harris, on the other hand, saw this as an attraction. "One of the things I find extremely endearing about him is how obvious his influences are. He doesn't try to say, 'Oh well it's kind of me, maybe it sounds a bit like someone else.' There they are, they're raw, all his influences are completely on the surface. He mixes and matches them, he uses them or he doesn't, or whatever . . ."

Other reviews – and they were surprisingly sparse, magazine editors plainly not connecting Ryan Adams with Whiskeytown – continued this theme of comparison with Dylan, Young and Parsons, leading to frustration for Ryan. "I hope that with time and perseverance people will stop saying that because it's really not the point," he told *Uncut*'s Nigel Williamson, one of his major champions in the UK press. "I'm looking forward to the day when somebody gets called the new Ryan Adams. I'll laugh to myself, give the guy a call and say, 'Don't worry about it.'"

Surprisingly, there'd been other songs of supposedly equal standard that, since they didn't fit the mood Ryan was seeking, did not make the final cut. "Continuity is important on a record," he'd explain, noting that there were two tracks in particular that, "Everyone (said), 'Why the fuck are you not putting them on?' One was very, very pop, and really could've been all kinds of things to people and maybe could have been on college radio. But look, thematically, it's not saying what everything else is saying."

Adams would reprise Whiskeytown's successful South By Southwest music festival performance of 1996 at the 2000 event, appearing alongside the likes of Roger McGuinn, Steve Forbert and David Gray. He played songs from *Heartbreaker* and revealed it would be released in September by Bloodshot, the Chicago label from which so much of the alt.country movement had flowed.

One of many fans he made at the event was singer-songwriter

Mike Kemp, preparing to record his own third album in Austin. It was his first time at South By Southwest – "the people I was with had been there before, coming back with all these tales of wonderful acts they'd seen" – and even though many of his heroes were playing in the tiny little bars and pubs, it would be Ryan Adams he'd take back with him as the dominant memory.

The opening night, called the Swollen Circus, took place in a tiny, little bar off the city's main street called the Hole in the Wall. "A few of the acts I knew of, most of them I didn't, but we were assured they were very good and they all proved to be," says Kemp. "Anyway, one-by-one these great acts kept coming up, but the buzz around the bar was, 'Ryan Adams is coming, Ryan Adams is coming, this is gonna be amazing.' I had never heard of this guy before, so asked my friends who he was. They told me he used to be in a band called Whiskeytown, who again I had never heard of. So before he'd even played, I'd turned off him! There was a big hype about him, and I was wondering, 'Why are all these people bothered about this guy when they've got these great talents here?'

"Somewhere towards the end of the evening there was a bit of a commotion at the door. Someone said, 'He's here, he's outside!' I looked out the window and there was a group of guys hanging around a scruffy-looking guy, who looked like a Greenwich Village-era Dylan. He was waving his arms about, and they seemed to be pleading with him. It turned out that he had turned up and, having looked inside the bar and seen how crowded it was, decided he didn't want to play. They were trying to talk him into playing, which they eventually did. So, after a small set-up, he got on this tiny little stage six inches off the ground and sat with his back to the audience smoking a cigarette, while they got his guitar ready. He was just rocking backwards and forwards like a little child that had been told off. Of course, by this time I hated him even more! (Laughs) I was like, 'What's going on with *you*?!'

"So he finally turned round to the audience and they all shouted titles of songs they wanted him to play. He said words to the effect that, 'I'm not going to play any of that shit' – the Whiskeytown stuff, obviously. 'This is a new song and it's about . . . oh fuck it, you don't care what it's about,' which didn't endear him to me much either. He then proceeded to play – I'm pretty sure, I'd had a few drinks by now – 'Sweet Carolina', after which you could hear sounds of jaws dropping around the bar . . . in complete and utter silence. I thought, 'Wow, now I *know* what all the fuss is about,' 'cos he was absolutely amazing."

Adams performed another three, maybe four songs before he left. Kemp saw him again two nights later at the Waterloo Brewing Company, another well-known Austin music venue when he went to see Alejandro Escovedo play and Adams turned up unannounced as a guest. "This time it was real hard-hitting rock'n'roll in a band situation. I'd seen Escovedo's band on a previous night at the Austin Music Awards when they'd played a tribute to Sterling Morrison from The Velvet Underground . . . a marvellous band. Ryan got up there and played a few songs."

He had played a solo gig the previous night, in between his Hole in the Wall appearance and Alejandro Escovedo, as special guest to Steve Earle. Earle had headlined the Stubbs Barbecue, one of the main events at SXSW, at a venue that held about 2,500 people – big by Austin standards. Earle was being supported by his Springsteen-esque protégés Marah, with a solo Adams the special surprise guest.

That night, so it's said, he got booed off stage by Steve Earle's crowd. Apparently he said something between songs to upset them – "they were very right-wing redneck, not the typical Ryan audience" – and he left the stage exclaiming, "That's it, I'm never playing again, I'll go home and kill myself and it'll be *your* fault" – to which, there were cheers of delight.

He had clearly bounced back within 24 hours and was keen to regain his confidence by playing second fiddle to Alejandro Escovedo, recapturing their partnership on the second Whiskeytown album. Indeed, Ryan would contribute vocals to Escovedo's 2001 release *A Man Under The Influence*, appearing on 'Don't Need You' and 'As I Fall'.

"I think Alejandro is a kind of father figure to him," says Kemp, "they get on well and (Ryan) was happy to let someone else have the spotlight. I didn't see him at Steve Earle but apparently he looked very uncomfortable, and he definitely did at the Hole in the

Wall gig where, although he was brilliant, he didn't look at ease at all. But when I saw him with Escovedo he looked like he had had a drink or two and he was really rocking; he was great that night.

"We saw him again the following night at a thing they call a 'songwriter in the round', which was in a small bar in Austin, just off 6th Street with Jim Lauderdale (who had just appeared on the Gram Parsons tribute album alongside Whiskeytown) and a few other local singer/songwriters. We'd actually gone to see someone else, but Ryan was there that night. He was in this line-up, there were five singer/songwriters and he went last. Jim Lauderdale started with one of his famous songs, 'King Of Broken Hearts', and they went through the songwriters one by one. Ryan played last but was plagued by technical problems; his guitar kept cutting out and his mic kept feeding back, but he persevered and he was *brilliant*.

"Two days later we ran into Jim Lauderdale in Dallas and told him we enjoyed the singer/songwriter thing. He asked us what we thought of Ryan Adams and we said, 'He was amazing; he's great, isn't he?' And Jim said, 'Yeah, he's something else. He's either going to be the biggest thing since Dylan, or dead.' I thought how right he was. He seemed to think that he had a lot of problems, I remember him saying the kid's screwed up or something. I think it was one of the low points of his life, Whiskeytown was just coming to an end, or things were not good within Whiskeytown if they ever were, and he was really looking at pursuing his solo stuff. The rest, as they say, is history.

"So that was his South By Southwest appearance. I'm not sure if he did any other gigs that year but he certainly seemed to be there all week for the festival, hanging out at different bars."

Was the material he played in Austin from *Heartbreaker*? "Definitely. I remember bits of the songs, and I remember one of them had a lot of swearing in it, I think that was 'Come Pick Me Up'. They were definitely the seeds of the early songs." Mike Kemp went home a believer, and when the album surfaced there would be many more.

It was decided at an early stage that *Heartbreaker* would be heavily promoted in Britain, and the man entrusted with that task was press officer Paddy Forwood. "I first started working on the record in late 2000, when Cooking Vinyl picked up the album from Bloodshot. Marketing Director Rob Collins and Martin Goldschmidt, the MD here, were sent the album, and we were all pretty excited that we could put out such a great record. We were also really excited because we thought he had real potential. You could tell he had 'something' that was a little bit special and this record was also superb. He had support from journalists at that stage, although it was from the specialist press, and when we started working it we had a great reaction especially from mags like *Uncut* and *Mojo* and the broadsheets, so it was a great record to work."

He first started working on the record in late 2000 when Ryan came over and they concentrated on getting features. The going, at first, was tough. "To start with there were a couple of people who were big supporters but the *Heartbreaker* record didn't really excite (the press) that much; it was only much later that they came on board when things started to happen. They were a bit late on it all, but they definitely had a couple of key people that kept banging on about Ryan, and saying, 'This guy's a genius,' that type of thing, but at that stage audiences at the gigs were 30-something blokes. He hadn't crossed over to the wider audience that I think more recent gigs have displayed; it really was a cult thing."

Someone who heard the record and felt it strike an immediate chord was Elton John. He called when Ryan was in London and suggested they meet up. The fact was that *Heartbreaker*'s basic, 'low-fi' production had reminded Elton of the core values of albums like *Madman Across The Water* and *Tumbleweed Connection* that had made his name as a singer-songwriter in the early Seventies.

"If I hadn't heard *Heartbreaker*, I'd probably be lost in over-production somewhere," John has said. "I was completely and utterly floored by the simplicity and beauty of the songs." He suited actions to words by returning to the basic band sound of early albums with his next release, *Songs From The West Coast* – and was rewarded with a career-reviving album which bore the frank dedication: "Thanks to Ryan Adams for making me want to do better."

Ryan in 2002. "I must have had a hangover for two years, but I've reached a point where I know how to take care of myself." (*Rex Features*)

Multi-instrumentalist Mike Daly with Ryan at one of Whiskeytown's two London gigs in May 1998. (*Redferns*)

Caitlin Cary reunites with a solo Ryan on home turf at Chapel Hill, NC's Cat's Cradle venue in December, 1999. (*Daniel Coston/Retna*)

Ryan on stage at Local 506, Chapel Hill in October 1999, working up some of the songs that would become *Heartbreaker*. (*Daniel Coston/Retna*)

Ryan with sometime girlfriend Leona Naess and Elton John on the Wizard of Oz-style set of the 'Answering Bell' video, January 2002. (*Bob Gruen/Star File*)

Ryan gets pally with Bob Dylan and the host of the 10th Annual Elton John AIDS Foundation Instyle Party in Hollywood, March 2002. (*Kevin Mazur/WireImage*)

That purrfect moment: the studio cat at New York's Electric Ladyland Studios gets the star treatment, August 2002. (*Bob Gruen/Star File*)

Above and below: Ryan on stage at the London Astoria, November 2001, a gig at which he also supported himself with an acoustic set despite an injured hand. (*Angela Lubrano*)

Ryan celebrates *New Musical Express's* half-century with a solo performance at London's Astoria, February 2002. (*Steve Gillett*)

Bridging the generation gap: Ryan shares the stage with Thom Yorke of Radiohead, James Taylor and Neil Young at a Bridge School benefit concert, California, October 2002. (*LFI*)

"As you get older, you realise screwing up doesn't seem to be an answer any longer." (*Bob Gruen/Star File*)

It wasn't the first time in recent months that Elton had bestowed his royal seal of approval on a contemporary artist, having duetted with the supposedly homophobic rapper Eminem at the 2001 Grammies. But nothing could devalue the compliment in Ryan's eyes. "What a sweetheart! I almost cried. But Elt is my buddy, he's so cool."

Ryan's tour in support of *Heartbreaker* saw him playing a series of solo shows that kicked off in Nashville on the first day of September 2000 and, after stopping off in Seattle to play the *No Depression* party, saw him spend a week 'at home' in Raleigh, playing dates at the Brewery and Chapel Hill's Local 506. From there, momentum gathered through Chicago, Detroit, Toronto, Philadelphia and Cambridge before a return to the Big Apple. He spent most of October in New York, having obviously exorcised his personal demons regarding the city, and girding his loins before the first solo tour of Europe.

Preparations for his visit had been both thorough and extensive. "We did an awful lot of stuff before he came over," remembers Paddy Forwood, "so there was more radio (than print) stuff (to do). I remember he had to do two questionnaires with *Mojo* and *Dazed And Confused*, and his answers were really kind of thoroughly thought out. He gave all the info he could and more, and they were really fascinating in-depth answers to the questions."

His gig at the Maze Club, Nottingham, on November 13 was the first at which he covered Oasis' 'Wonderwall', and something that happened off stage inspired a song he'd perform once only called 'Dear Thief'. It was directed at the person (fan or otherwise) who'd taken his precious notebook full of song lyrics. Deciding that writing a song about it would be the most direct form of action, he sang 'Dear Thief' the following night . . . and was re-united with his notebook 24 hours later.

Three days later he returned to the Borderline in London, scene of Whiskeytown's two-night triumph a couple of years previously. The solo show, he admitted, was rather more low-key than on that occasion. "I get really quiet and I don't play with a pick or anything. I don't stand up, I sit down in a chair and just like get sort of lost, and people usually follow." Audience members even seemed to know songs that didn't even make the record, "songs I just play live that I've been playing since I started doing my own thing."

Paddy Forwood was a more than interested onlooker, and believed the solo Ryan compared favourably with what he'd seen of him with Whiskeytown. "In a way it was more intense, it was a better show in terms that it was literally him, and it was more impressive that he could command such attention. He had the audience literally eating out of his hand, it was really a brilliant, brilliant show. He had an instant rapport with the audience, a charisma which you can't fake and obviously beautiful songs, and he wasn't shy of trying things out. He got on the piano a couple of times and just would say, 'I wrote this yesterday,' or 'this afternoon, I'll give it a go,' and still sound fantastic.

"I've seen the later shows both solo and with a band and he was a lot more tuned in with the music side of things than at earlier gigs, and seemed in the later gigs to have the in-between song banter and that whole persona. But at that stage it was a really good balance of a lot of songs and a lot of music but with the self-deprecating humour and piss-taking and that kind of thing, the dishevelled look – always playing with his hair and stuff and chainsmoking."

The dishevelled look apparently came without artifice. "It's kind of natural; when he's not at a gig he looks exactly the same. He was just an awesome performer."

The solo gigs saw people calling for Whiskeytown material to be played – something Ryan resisted with good reason, Forwood suggested. "OK, he doesn't play anything from his (Whiskeytown) back catalogue, but you just got the impression that he had so much material to play, especially new stuff. What he was really into was what he was writing at that moment, but he did play a lot of the *Heartbreaker* stuff which was quite good in terms of playing songs from the record that he was promoting. But I think even at that stage he'd already written a lot of new stuff."

Bob Harris had championed Adams since their meeting at the GLR radio station, and had now transferred to national BBC Radio 2. He played all the broadcastable *Heartbreaker* tracks on his show and, having turned on many listeners to the album, received "a fair amount of correspondence from people who are fascinated by the notebooks Ryan has on stage and the way that he has with him. Being up there solo on stage it's all going to be exposed even more."

Having announced himself as a major talent, the music press and the cult following he had amassed helped Ryan Adams' UK reputation take off gradually over the next year. "Elton John got to hear about *Heartbreaker* a little while after it was released," Paddy Forwood recalls, "but it did seem a lot of influential people were talking about it, saying it was the album of the year and that kind of thing. I know that Jeff Barrett (Heavenly Records) was really into it. It was a real word of mouth thing: 'You've got to check this guy out.'

"It felt quite organic," he continues, "because there was no hype at all. We didn't push Ryan in people's faces – we didn't need to, his music was good enough to work on its own. It sort of snowballed. By the time of the Lyric gigs he'd just signed to Universal and was on Lost Highway, which was part of that deal. At that stage (present UK publicist) Richard Wootton took over. He'd looked after him originally (in Whiskeytown), so it was kind of natural."

In summary, Ryan Adams had more than lived up to his press agent's expectations. "He was just a cool guy, really. I think he was a little bit apprehensive before the gigs as they were his first UK live solo shows, especially at the Borderline, but I thought he was a really nice guy."

At that point, Ryan later confessed, his self-esteem needed a boost, and the album's success took him completely by surprise. "I had no idea," he admits. "I expected the thing to sell, like, 3,000 copies. I didn't think anybody knew me any more." By the time he got back from Europe, it had blown up "to a level that indie records don't – any more, anyway. It was pretty legitimate. Everyone was like, 'Man, when you get back you're not gonna believe it.' I'm like, 'Oh, don't try and make me feel better.' Optimist that I am."

Having toured *Heartbreaker* solo, Ryan decided his next move would be to record a cutting-edge rock album – and that meant putting himself back into a band situation. "I figure I'll be 27 this year, and it's high time I actually made a youthful rock'n'roll record . . . I've never had a chance to get behind the electric guitar and make it work for me for a whole record. I've gotta make one record that's funny and about being in your twenties, because I've spent my twenties writing songs like I'm 47."

His vehicle, combining the best elements of Hüsker Dü, The Replacements and The Stones, would be a band recruited from the ever-teeming pool of Nashville hopefuls in the autumn of 2000. The line-up consisted of a quartet of musicians, bassist Billy Mercer (who had played with Kim Richey and Nick Kane), drummer Brad Pemberton (Patty Griffin, Iodine) and, for a short while, John Paul Keith, who'd played together in an outfit called Stateside.

Singer, songwriter and guitarist Keith, a 27-year-old native of Knoxville, Tennessee, had considerable previous form. In many respects, in fact, his career paralleled Adams. As a teenager he was a founding member of The Viceroys, who later renamed themselves The V-Roys, but had left the band before they signed to Steve Earle's E Squared label. He relocated to Nashville and formed the Nevers, who quickly landed a major-label deal with Sire Records but, as with Whiskeytown, got lost in corporate restructuring.

Keith had put Stateside together in 2000, and the quartet had been playing together around Nashville for some while, initially under his name. His musical manifesto was "to take classic Tom Petty-style songwriting and give it a more modern, Foo Fighters-type, big guitar sound." Stateside soon hit the studio, completing *Twice As Gone* for indie label Disgraceland Records, the energetic album (complete with a backing vocal guest appearance from Ryan Adams on 'Little Black Dress') drawing comparisons with Tom Petty, The Rolling Stones, The Replacements and British Invasion pop.

The chemistry between singer and group was immediate ("it was just kinda like BAM!", enthused Ryan) and they started playing shows within a week of forming. But Keith had ambitions of his own, quitting early on to form a new line-up of Stateside which came together in summer 2002 in Birmingham, Alabama. He would be replaced by a familiar name: Brad Rice, the guitarist who had appeared in the latter stages of the Whiskeytown story and had since shown up both on the Gram Parsons tribute and an album, *Southern Lines*, by The Backsliders.

The addition of multi-instrumentalist Bucky Baxter, an older character who'd first come to Nashville in 1977 before gaining considerable recording and touring experience with artists as well known as Steve Earle, Steve Forbert and Bob Dylan, would have the kind of gelling effect Mike Daly's recruitment had given Whiskeytown, and his ability to cover both steel, acoustic and electric guitars would prove invaluable.

In 1988, when Baxter was working with Steve Earle on his *Copperhead Road* album in Memphis, Michael Stipe had invited him to sit in on a *Green* recording session. He'd switched allegiance to Dylan in 1992 as Steve Earle's personal problems saw him jailed and in detox, performing with Bob on MTV's *Unplugged* in 1995 and recording *Time Out Of Mind* before returning to Nashville in 1998.

Soon after the new band's line-up solidified, they went into the studio and recorded "a quick, loud and sloppy 10-song, 40-minute record" with Dave Domanich (of Lenny Kravitz fame) producing. 'Wonderwall' made a reappearance, while the original 'Song For Keith Richards' featured saxophone from sometime Rolling Stones sideman Bobby Keys. Other seemingly jokey titles included 'Tennessee Sucks' and 'I Took Your Puppies To The Racetrack'.

"The songs just sorta fell out of my coat," said Ryan, who revealed he'd first encountered bassist Mercer serving on the other side of a bar. (Temporary jobs were a necessary evil for those trying to gain a precarious foothold in Music City.) "As rock as we are," he enthused about his new band, "we're gonna stay rock, but it's going to get a little more psychedelic, like The Flaming Lips. I want to utilise those three guitars a little bit more. Keep that edgy rock'n'roll happening, but then throw some art in there." Humour, too. "It's really, really funny – not total joke songs, but songs where we're really just having a great time. You can hear the humour, and it was a really laid-back thing."

The quartet would, in time, mutate into Ryan's regular backing band, picking up the names LAX and then the Sweetheart

Revolution along the way before becoming The Pinkhearts – a name originally reserved for their 'punk/garage' style recordings. Yet despite having made a great album and found a band in Nashville during 2000, Adams' next musical move would take shape not in Music City but Los Angeles.

8

Striking Gold In LA

IT WAS CLEAR from the moment *Heartbreaker*'s first sales figures rolled in that Ryan Adams wouldn't be spending the rest of his life on an independent label. (Indeed, he'd had the foresight to sign a one-album deal only with Bloodshot.) It could hardly have been predicted, though, that he'd return to a relationship with the music business conglomerate that had delayed *Pneumonia*'s release. But it would be at one important remove.

Lost Highway was indeed part of the Universal Music Group, but by the time of Adams' signing had built a roster that included such names as Lucinda Williams and Willie Nelson. It had snagged soundtrack rights to the mega-hit music movie *O Brother, Where Art Thou?*, starring George Clooney, which had accomplished the task of making country hip for at least two minutes (the CD selling six million in the process), while the label's Hank Williams tribute album *Timeless* featured Adams alongside such stellar names as Dylan, Beck, Mark Knopfler and Keith Richards, all paying tribute to the late, great country songwriter.

"There was no A&R interference whatsoever," said co-producer Mary Martin. "The artists chose the songs. Everybody was given the same amount of money for recording costs. We told them to go off and have a good time." Ryan's choice was 'Lovesick Blues', a suitable title for a man whose tangled love life seemed to feed his muse. It would also, in time, win him a share in a Grammy.

Lost Highway Records was founded by Luke Lewis, a 55-year-old music-business veteran who, coincidentally, went to high school with Gram Parsons but, probably more importantly, was an Adams fan before he signed him to a solo contract. He had, in fact, been chairman of the very successful Mercury Nashville label, and his career had been caught in the self-same boardroom shuffle that had put Whiskeytown's last album into suspended animation.

Lewis was savvy enough to know that Adams could be sold to two different age groups – his own, who would key into the Gram Parsons/Rolling Stones references, and a younger, more impressionable clientele. "I knew my generation would like this music but what really sold me was when my kids, who are 20 and 22 and into rap, responded to it. I felt a generational connection. Ryan is a bit of a rebel, a new breed. He was raised on punk, but he has a sense of the songwriting tradition. Plus, he's got more energy than anyone I've ever seen."

The artist himself was delighted. "I have people now that say, 'That kid loves to make music. Let's let him make music: let's keep the overhead low and let him go,'" he said of Lost Highway. But there were no regrets about his association with Outpost. "I got godawful amounts of money; haven't worked since I was 19," he said. "No matter what happened, it was, 'Thank you for paying me for doing nothing.' I ended up in the best place I could have," Adams concluded.

While some might have expected the once-bitten singer to go his own way, Paddy Forwood, his former UK press agent, wasn't surprised that he signed up to the 'beast' once more. "You kind of felt with Ryan that his eye was on the bigger game, really; he loved his music and there was no 'hey I want to be an indie star'. I think he just wanted to sell as many records as he could, and his music was for all to hear, not just a privileged few."

The key to the deal was that Adams' manager, Frank Callari, combined that job with the post of senior vice president of A&R for the label. Yet this development obviously meant that Cooking Vinyl, Bloodshot's licensees, lost Ryan for the UK. "It was a real shame that we couldn't carry on working with him," said Forwood, "but it was a fairly obvious move for Ryan to go wherever (his manager) was going to go."

Adams had initially refused to specify which label he'd be signing with, though he revealed it would also be releasing Whiskeytown's long lost *Pneumonia* project as part of the package. "I don't want to jinx it," he explained of both his move and the release, although he went as far as describing his new home as "the outlaw major. Some people are starting something new that's going to kick the ass of all these bullshit, Seagrams-owned record companies."

Having decided to take a fortnight's break in Los Angeles during Christmas 2000 as a present to himself, Ryan Adams decided on a whim to put his possessions into storage and relocate to the West Coast, where he found the locals both friendly and receptive to this perennial outsider. Besides, "Nashville was eating me alive."

It hadn't been a hard decision to make; given the desperation of the previous winter, the last thing he wanted to be was alone. "I was living by myself in a two-storey house with a studio in the basement, and all my room-mates had left while I was on tour. So I came back and thought, this really *sucks*. Nashville winters are long and tremendous, and New York is worse. I actually left Nashville when it was snowing, and it was so bad that everyone's locks would freeze on their cars."

He certainly changed his lifestyle to make more of the daytime, professing to enjoy "getting up at 11 o'clock in the morning: the sun is out every day, you can walk outside and it's really nice . . . it's changed my personality." It also changed the shape of his next record, which he'd originally intended to be "Roy Orbison-type dark" – in other words, as dark, if not darker, than *Heartbreaker*. "And I branched off. I decided I was gonna write songs about other people, make paintings about things I didn't know about, as opposed to just another record about me."

Not that he'd forsaken the night life totally, taking pleasure in exploring the network of small clubs situated behind Hollywood Boulevard which came alive after the sun went down. "Los Angeles has a strange, particular vibe to it," he'd explain enthusiastically. "I totally see what the Doors were on about when I'm out there . . . it's one of the nicest places in the States in terms of people being friendly. Everywhere else, you're just a fuckin' stranger."

It was in this environment that he'd encountered some "really cool people", among them a kindred singer-songwriter in the shape of dreadlocked Adam Duritz. The Counting Crows singer, who'd enjoyed a similar cult status to Ryan without breaking through to the musical mainstream, would become a valued friend and collaborator in the months ahead.

Another ray of sunlight hit Adams' life in the shape of actress Winona Ryder, potentially the last piece in the West Coast jigsaw: "I met somebody, and that was it," he'd said enigmatically. Ryder, at 29 three years older than the singer, was considered one of the most accomplished actresses around, with hit movies like *Beetlejuice, Bram Stoker's Dracula* and *Alien: Resurrection* to her name, not to mention two Oscar nominations for her work in *The Age Of Innocence* and *Little Women.* Yet her love life, appearing without exception to involve famous musicians and actors, had made her the subject of almost as much publicity as her screen work.

After ending her engagement to screen star Johnny Depp, she was romantically linked to several celebrities in succession, including David Duchovny, Paul Westerberg (of Replacements fame) and Daniel Day-Lewis. Her most public relationship with a rock star was with Soul Asylum lead singer Dave Pirner. In 1998, after that had ended, Winona became romantically involved with actor Matt Damon and they moved in together. That broke up in 2000, leaving her free to pursue her interest in Ryan – and vice versa.

Interestingly, the pair could have got together after Whiskeytown's ill-fated Fillmore gig, but Ryan had reportedly turned down her request to come backstage with a curt, "No, thanks! What was I *supposed* to say?" he'd protested at the time. "I mean, I have a girlfriend . . . Anyway, I have no interest in being a rock star. I just want to make the perfect music. And I never want to sell it out. It's not about me getting to sit next to (Jane's Addiction/Red Hot Chili Peppers' guitarist) Dave Navarro at some awards show."

The situation was clearly different now, and Adams would explain that his forthcoming album, to be entitled *Gold*, was meant as an open letter for "this one other person in the entire world, who shall go unnamed; the record's for her – not that she cares." He rather spoilt the secret by citing Winona in the liner notes. "Ryan loves just about everybody, including . . . Winona Ryder – damn girl." That said, he managed to name-check Alanis Morrisette five times among the other names!

He later elaborated somewhat harshly on the Ryder situation. "I made an ignorant choice of girlfriend. I met this famous person and thought, 'I'll date her!' I'd been in a relationship since I was 17, so I'd never had a chance to be a guy, and I don't know how to be a bachelor and go out and have fun. But all we did was torture each other, it was really silly. I don't know what I was doing with her in the first place."

Adams certainly seemed to emerge from the relationship with the better hand. He'd end 2001 with three Grammy nominations including Best Male Rock Vocal Performance for 'New York, New York', Best Rock Album for *Gold* and Best Country Male Vocal for 'Lovesick Blues' from the Hank Williams tribute album *Timeless*.

Winona's world view was certainly nowhere near as rosy. That December would see her arrested for grand theft when she was alleged to have shoplifted over $4,000 worth of clothes, while at the same time she was charged with illegal possession of prescription drugs. She was later charged with four felonies – theft, burglary, vandalism, and possession of a controlled substance – but pleaded innocent to all charges. (She was found guilty of theft and vandalism in November 2002.)

The nature of the relationship between Ryan and Ryder was never to be fully clarified – but, on one occasion when playing 'The Bar Is A Beautiful Place' in the UK the following year, Adams changed a single, significant word of the last verse, inserting 'Miss Horowitz' (the actress' real surname) in place of the usual 'Miss Samuels'.

Still in Britain, his late-April '01 show at Newcastle's Live Theatre was poorly reviewed by local magazine *Get Rhythm*, which accused him of acting like a sixteen-year-old, and that a sell-out crowd in a venue that could have been filled four times had been well and truly short-changed. "He showed little respect," the reviewer complained. "For the first 40 minutes it was like he was going through an act of his own."

Someone in the audience pulled him up on the time he was spending drinking as opposed to singing, and this clearly hit a raw nerve as he departed the stage without either a backward glance or an encore. "He left us to reflect on his surreal performance with low lights, low sound, no interviews and no flash photography . . . memories will linger longer for what he might have achieved rather than did."

Two London shows at Hammersmith's Lyric Theatre saw him draw, by and large, a more star-struck crowd, even on a Monday night. But his initially grumpy hungover demeanour and complaint that "my songs are even bumming me out" suggested an irascible Tom Waits-style character lurking inside a rather younger body. The stage was typically bare, with two chairs, a piano and, inevitably, a notebook. Nevertheless, clutching a spirit glass and an acoustic guitar, Adams opened up both personally and musically as the evening went on. An opening cover of Oasis' 'Wonderwall' was unexpected to many, but the train lurched back on a more predictable track.

He was joined for the closing 'Come Pick Me Up' by Carina Round, his choice as the night's essential Kim Richey substitute on that show-stopping song (and presumably the inspiration for the still-unreleased 'A Song For Carina'). Round, born in a deprived area of Wolverhampton, had toured with the likes of David Gray, Miles Hunt and Mark Eitzel. It's not certain how she and Ryan met, but their backgrounds (brought up by mother, close relationship with grandparent) seemed strangely similar.

On his Birmingham date on the tour on May 1 the pair wrote a song, 'The Idiot Dance', in the dressing room and performed it that night – but on this occasion she was happy to be a bit-part player. (The new song was played on four other occasions in May, but does not appear on Round's album, *The First Blood Mystery*.) Support singer Sally Timms could also boast an Adams connection, performing an unreleased composition of his called 'Out Of Touch'.

The show's format was something he'd clearly thought deeply about. "I'm always going to be playing current stuff," he answered to the suggestion that he could have given some of the *Pneumonia* material an airing. "They're on the record, and that's over. I don't play a single Whiskeytown song in my solo show. Half of the show, one hour of the two hours I played, was new songs. I play until curfew, then I'm beat and have to be dragged off."

He equally rejected the idea of concentrating on the album he was supposed to be promoting. "I write songs how other people write in their journal: it's how I make sense of the world. So it doesn't make any sense for me to throw out a record and then tour it for a year. I'll always be playing songs, so who cares if they're new or old?" 'Dear Anne', a song inspired by World War II heroine Anne Frank's diary, which he'd written and premiered on tour in Sweden earlier that month, began the encore. (Though widely bootlegged, it would soon fall from the repertoire and has yet to turn up on any official release.)

Not everybody in the Hammersmith audience was on his side 100 per cent, particularly after a burst of semi-obscene between-song patter. The aside, "It's my party and I'll wank if I want to . . ." was greeted by the barely more polite enquiry from an audience member: "What's it like up your own ass?" The response, a curt "piss off!" seemed to bring him to reluctant life.

Reminded of this exchange a couple of days later, he made the distinction that, while he didn't take himself particularly seriously, "I take the songs really seriously." This would lead to comparisons with the likes of Loudon Wainwright III, whose between-song monologues eventually came to rival his music – probably to the detriment of his career prospects. (For the record, Adams managed to perform 16 numbers, despite the length of his soliloquies.)

The lovelorn tone of the album he was (supposed to be) promoting was a snapshot of a heartbroken man – but Adams warned its successor would not be 'son of'. "At the moment I made *Heartbreaker*, I was really distraught. If people end up thinking that *Heartbreaker* is the stock of what's in my soup, they are going to be really shocked when I throw peanut butter in. I can get really *goofy*."

Meanwhile, Ryan had discarded the double album's worth of songs he'd written "out of excitement" immediately on arriving in LA and recorded with Bucky Baxter. Few would make *Gold*'s final track listing, the vibe being compared with Bob Dylan's understated Seventies classic *Blood On The Tracks*. To qualify, the songs eventually chosen "had to work completely and honestly by themselves on acoustic guitar or on piano. If they didn't, they weren't worth putting on the record." This still-born venture was to become known as *The Suicide Handbook*.

So many new songs were flowing from Adams' charged pen that a double (vinyl) album format still seemed the most likely result. The first disc would be New York-themed before Nashville and LA claimed a (vinyl) side apiece. Songs would end up being shifted around to improve the flow of the record, but a hint of the original concept remained with 'New York, New York', the opener, and 'Goodnight, Hollywood Blvd', the final track.

Room had been found for 16 new songs, which had been pared down from 26 when he doubted his audience had the patience to listen to one CD with 16 songs on it, let alone two. "I decided that it should be one CD with enough songs to fit on two vinyl LPs . . . and figured I'd hold onto that (extra) stuff for later." The double vinyl format had been beloved by him since the Rolling Stones' *Exile On Main Street*, a formative album of his youth (even if it was released two years before he was born!). Among the new songs rejected was '1974', written with Alanis Morrisette (who just happened to share Ryan's year of birth).

This time round, the introspective, downbeat vibe of *Heartbreaker* would be replaced by a more mainstream approach. "This might not be exactly alt.country," said *Country Music International*, "nor could it be termed mainstream country, but *Gold* has a lot of musical merit, as long as you're not repelled by simply-presented songs about deeper things than you're likely to hear on country radio these days."

The shimmering confidence *Gold* exuded reflected the fact that Adams was happier in his skin than ever before – something he described as "a symptom of growing up. I can make a little bit more sense of the world. I have more to base stuff on, and I can compare things better. My palette has gained 18 more colours, and I've taken the time to check them out."

There was to be no repeat of the emotional turmoil of *Heartbreaker*, a record he admitted had been "hard to make. It was so emotional, and I was a little frazzled. With *Gold*, I was ready to lift myself up and make some emotional judgements on things." The upbeat tone, he admitted, hadn't been a bad idea "considering I already made a really bummer record. But I was on my way to making another bummer record (in *The Suicide Handbook*), and it didn't come out like that."

If *Heartbreaker* was Adams' New York album, dealing with a lost love there, then *Gold* could qualify as his take on Los Angeles: "Gold is what the buildings and streets look like in LA when the sun goes down." The album cover certainly couldn't have been more different when compared with its predecessor's studied ennui. Rather than having some kind of *Hotel California*-style West Coast image, it went the other way entirely and appeared to offer a remix of Bruce Springsteen's *Born In The USA* theme from nearly two decades earlier.

The full-frame cover photo juxtaposed Adams with an upside-down American flag – a fact that would take on an added (and unwanted) significance in the wake of the September 11 World Trade Centre and Pentagon attacks that took place two weeks before release.

Its seemingly patriotic theme appears to have struck a chord with people looking for some hope or solace after the biggest peacetime disaster the nation had ever known, while the single 'New York, New York' would become an anthem. But fearful of being seen to be inappropriate, Ryan felt strongly enough to make his feelings and motives clear to his fans in the following web message:

"I have been recently delivered back to my New York City, beautiful, beloved, and dear city it is . . . Our world has been changed, and our lives have been affected and peace has been put in jeopardy. It's difficult not to feel numb. The people I do not even know who I passed on the street yesterday, at some point looking down the avenue to only smoke . . . My prayers and my heart are with everyone in loss. We are all at loss. And my support is with everyone fighting to save lives, and honour peace, and uplift those who cannot . . . So to anyone out there, I say hold on, and hold your friends up and don't stop. Not for anyone.

"I'm gonna walk down my block and go to the places I always go and call my friends, and live my life and rise above this. RISE ABOVE what others couldn't. These are hard things to communicate, these are dire times, and rock and roll seems silly. The way things that bugged my friends about their lives or this country seem silly now . . . seem unimportant. Those differences are OURS.

"Because this is where we live. This is where we decide what changes. This is where we find our peace. And somebody messed with that. Took the locks off our doors. They're not gonna take the locks off my heart, and they're not gonna take my friends from me, the ones we have here and now."

The 'Old Glory' cover to the album had actually been selected from a choice of two, the second picturing him bending over an old-fashioned record player; another shot from that session appears on the back page of the CD booklet, while both record player and flag (right way up this time) are on the back tray liner. The reason for his choice of cover image, he told the *New York Times*, was that it looked "powerful . . . I also kind of wanted to tweak the whole Bruce Springsteen *Born In The USA* thing. Instead of me standing there all tough like Bruce, I'm in slouchy, twitchy posture, my head down, my hair a mess. We thought it looked cool, but it was also meant to be a bit of a goof." He wasn't out, he insisted, to court popularity through perceived patriotism. "The crowds have been real loving. I hope it's not for that reason. I hope it's because they dig the music."

The packaging broke with tradition by featuring the songs' lyrics – a first for Ryan in either Whiskeytown or solo days – which also suggested an added degree of self-confidence. The album had come together at Sunset Sound studio in Hollywood late in the spring of 2001, with Ethan Johns at the controls as usual. He'd resisted the temptation to bring his new backing band into the studio, instead using bassists Jennifer Condos (familiar from the last knockings of Whiskeytown) and Milo De Cruz plus Chris Stills on guitar and vocals "filling in the blanks".

Keyboards were played by both Benmont Tench, of Tom Petty's Heartbreakers and Richard Causon – another *Pneumonia* sideman, who'd go on to play with Ryan-related artists Alanis Morissette and Julianna Raye – while a slew of backing vocalists featured included pal Adam Duritz and two female singer protégées of Ethan Johns. CeeCee White had co-fronted a band with Chris Stills in which Ethan had played drums, while the previously mentioned Julianna Raye had been 'discovered' eight years earlier when she had "played me a few songs on a piano late one evening and I was astounded." (She would record a début album for his embryonic 3 Crows Music label.) Everything else except brass was covered by the ever-dependable Johns himself.

Adams had recently spent time listening to solo singer-songwriters like James Taylor, bluesman John Hammond, and "all that Keith (Richards) stuff, all that great *Beggars Banquet*-style acoustic rhythm (guitars)." The songs were, as usual, written on acoustic but, for the first time since *Strangers Almanac*, he used a pick when playing. This, some have suggested, may explain why the album is strikingly upbeat compared to either *Heartbreaker* or *Pneumonia*, both of which were apparently written in his New York apartment using his fingers and thumb to strum at low volume to avoid upsetting the neighbours.

But if he'd entered the studio with the germ of a musical idea, lyrics and other details were left until the last minute. Photocopies would be passed around and the result was usually a first or second take. "I want people to come up with their own ideas and interpretations," he explained of this policy. And the white heat of creativity was welcomed by all involved. "It's like, 'There it is. Goddamit, this is shit-hot, right now this is what I'm feeling, this is just off the press.' If it's like, 'Well, I could've done the C-section better,' you're like, 'Too late. The moment was there.' My voice was either there or not; if it was there half the song, then fine."

The single 'New York, New York' kicked off in style with a mix of Hammond organ, acoustic guitar and hand percussion reminiscent of Eric Clapton in laid-back *461 Ocean Boulevard* mode. 'Had myself a lover finer than gold/But I've broken up and busted up since' ran the autobiographical lyric, while instrumentally the track was almost a one-man show with Ethan Johns on guitar, organ, drums and congas. This was to be followed up by another stormer in 'Firecracker', Dylanesque harmonica setting an upbeat mood from the off and a nod to Neil Young's *Rust Never Sleeps* in the 'I wanna burn up hard and bright' chorus refrain.

'Answering Bell', the eventual second single, was so reminiscent of early-Seventies *Tupelo Honey*-era Van Morrison – especially in its middle eight – that Adams became tired of rebutting the accusation. "*Everybody* says that, but I don't own any Van Morrison records! I was just trying to do some white-boy soul." The self-played banjo-led intro, too, nodded to The Band before Pinkheart Bucky Baxter weighed in with some sweetly stinging steel.

The enigmatic title of 'La Cienega Just Smiled' comes from a moment when he stood on the corner of Los Angeles' La Cienega Boulevard and Melrose Avenue reflecting on his recent past. There's a vocal resemblance to David Gray and an almost metronomic propulsion that also echoes the *White Ladder* man as the mood of the album lurches downbeat for the first time.

'The Rescue Blues' had in fact been in the live set as a slower-paced piano and vocal song since September 2000: the bootleg *Silver And Gold* contains a studio demo version recorded around that time. Turn the clock on a year and Ryan's performances with his band turned it into something altogether different, substituting full-on guitars for piano. In January 2002, the song was revamped again with a blues-based opening and ending sandwiching the 'rock' centre-section. The album version falls somewhere in the middle. 'Somehow, Someday' is a faster homage to The Band's 'The Weight', allied with a *Comes A Time* Neil Young vocal. But there also comes a time when the listener tires of citing the similarities and, surrendering, starts enjoying the album for what it is.

'When The Stars Go Blue', the album's outstanding ballad, came together in just a few songwriting minutes. Compared with *Heartbreaker*, in which he was "beating myself up over things or feelings", *Gold* found "some of the awkwardness gone. And some of the questions I had to ask are a little bit gone." A Morrissey-esque vocal completed the portrait of despair which evoked Roy Orbison's Sixties tales of harrowing emotion. The 'stars' reference has a deeper meaning, according to the writer. "Think of the 'star' as someone hiding away in her Beverly Hills mansion and not saying an awful lot," he says. "Listen to the song again with that in mind and see what you think."

The song's combination of a string section, keyboards and backing vocals by Julianna Raye make the song, written early in

2001, particularly noteworthy. Other ears recognised its majesty when Irish female family group The Corrs immediately placed a cover version in their set – and invited U2's Bono to join them in its performance on the live album *VH1 Presents: The Corrs Live In Dublin*, the most high-profile Ryan Adams cover yet to find release.

At some nine minutes long, 'Nobody Girl' seemed to be the song that polarised fans, sorting the dedicated from the discerning. "Pete Townshend playing Steve Cropper fills," said *Guitar* magazine with a weather eye on the axe influences. Others fingered The Band's 'The Weight' yet again, this mutating into Traffic's post-psychedelic classic 'Dear Mr Fantasy' via a Keith Richards-style guitar solo. One reviewer suggested the omission of this sprawling track plus the two songs that followed would have tightened things up and produced a more cohesive *Gold* – but there are many that would disagree.

The title of track nine, 'Sylvia Plath' should in fact be 'SYLVIA PLATH' as it is the typographical equivalent of *Heartbreaker*'s 'AMY' but though Adams is still fantasising over an unattainable figure over a piano and strings backing, this time it's the suicide poet. "I'll leave the comparison open for you to decide" was his only comment. 'Enemy Fire', a guitar-driven mid-pacer slightly reminiscent of the Black Crowes in their moodier moments, was written by Ryan and Gillian Welch well over a year before the record-buying public heard it. Its first known performance was in June 2000 and, with its negligible lyrical content, had done well to make the cut.

The 'Pinball Wizard'-style opening chords of 'Gonna Make You Love Me' echoed the album's opener. But this joyous song – sample lyric 'Faith can keep you warm/But I'll teach you how to shake' – owed its Spanish rhythms and imagery to a trip Adams and his band had taken to Cancún, Mexico.

With its dead-slow pace, 'Wild Flowers' was always going to face comparison with The Stones' 'Wild Horses' and 'Dead Flowers'. Starting starkly, it built to a less substantial ending than could be hoped for, though the cleverly picked motif from 'Satisfaction' on acoustic guitar was a clever touch. The reedy, Neil Young-style vocal of 'Harder Now That It's Over' seemed to describe another dysfunctional, even violent relationship. 'I'm sorry' was the repeated refrain.

Despite its brass-laden studio arrangement, 'Touch, Feel & Lose' is a song Ryan has been as at home with playing solo as with a band. The co-writing credit with David Rawlings suggested it belonged with 'Enemy Fire' as a *Heartbreaker* hangover, though bootleg live versions only date from early 2001.

'Tina Toledo's Street Walkin' Blues' took the Rolling Stones fixation on a step, with CeeCee White trading vocal lines with Adams in the style of Merry Clayton on 'Gimme Shelter' as well as providing the album with its title in the repeated 'Silver and gold' refrain.

The subject of the song, Ryan revealed, was "a prostitute who was saving money to go to medical school, and the character needed a really ass-shaking fun vibe." This tip of the hat, he confessed, was purely unoriginal: "I don't pretend to have invented a thing," he says, and to prove it regularly drops in verses of the Stones' 'Midnight Rambler' and 'Can't You Hear Me Knocking' into his live renditions of the song which, while breaking the six-minute barrier in the studio, has often been stretched out in concert to as long as 15 minutes.

The show closed in highly satisfactory style with 'Goodnight, Hollywood Blvd', a reflective piano ballad with string accompaniment that needs little analysis.

Very different to *Heartbreaker, Gold* showed "the process of forgiving myself" was well under way. "It's more upbeat because I think I'm giving myself some air to breathe. I'm giving myself a chance to look at everything around me and not just be the victim. A lot of the subject matter is more of me describing things as . . . the emotions I feel."

The first 75,000 copies of the album included a bonus disc containing five tracks released in demo-sounding versions that arguably lacked the depth of production of the main event but were well worth fans' time. They also appeared as side four on a limited edition vinyl double LP, each track having been written during the album sessions. Julianna Raye and Adam Duritz featured on vocals with Johns, Stills and Adams, while the legendary Jim Keltner featured on drums – a feather in Ryan's cap.

'Rosalie Come And Go' duplicated 'New York, New York' in feel if not in sentiment, while 'The Fools We Are As Men' was a moody, low-fi masterpiece and 'Sweet Black Magic' – a rare Adams/Johns co-write – was almost straight country. 'Cannonball Days', with its lascivious lyric, was vaguely Dylanesque without sticking in the memory.

'The Bar Is A Beautiful Place', which would prove to be the most performed of these interlopers, was created in classic Ryan Adams style when he went bar-hopping one night on Hollywood Boulevard with the intention of finding inspiration for a few songs. When he came home the next morning he found songwords he couldn't remember writing scribbled on napkins, but nevertheless put them to music.

The package contained a massive amount of music for even the most die-hard fan to digest, but that wasn't the end of the story – not by a long chalk. The single 'New York, New York' had contained two bonus tracks in 'Mara Lisa' and 'From Me To You', bringing the total officially available tracks from the *Gold* sessions to 23. 'Mara Lisa' was very reminiscent of Bob Dylan's *Freewheeling* era, a sparse acoustic tale of love and life that really shouldn't have been thrown away as a B-side. 'From Me To You' was not a cover of the early Beatles classic but a love song that again would have made a lesser artist's album with ease.

It was a sobering thought (no pun intended) that, including *Heartbreaker, Gold, Pneumonia* and the CD single, over 50 new Ryan Adams songs had been exposed to the public at large within a year – testament to his productivity. Only two tracks originally leaked as *Gold* inclusions had slipped through the net: 'Off Broadway' (currently unavailable) and 'Dear Chicago', a version of which would surface on the following year's *Demolition* collection.

In keeping with Ryan's booze and fags image, a poster advertising the album showed him holding a wine bottle as he jumped in the air. The bottle was airbrushed out in certain territories, France, ironically, among them.

British newspapers and magazines were unanimous in acclaiming

Gold. Both the *Guardian* and the *Observer* made it their CD of the week, while rave reviews extended from tabloids like the *Mail* and *Mirror* to lads' mag *Loaded*. But as well as attempting not to analyse what he writes, Ryan had vowed not to read his own press. "I just want to make it and not fuss about it. No excuses for it. Just make it and there it is. That way, the process is more pure. And even if people hate it, well, it doesn't matter. Because I'm just doing it to do it."

The first dozen North American dates supporting the release of *Gold* in late September 2001 came interspersed with television appearances on such well-known national showcases as *The Late Show With David Letterman*. While a show in Boston would see Adam Duritz sitting in on harmony vocals (not to mention an impromptu 'Nervous Breakdown', still Ryan's fave punk cover), the second of two New York dates at the Irving Plaza in early October would feature a guest appearance from Elton John, an event guaranteed to get Adams' name in the headlines.

And this was to be no brief cameo, either: the pair democratically chose to perform a song apiece in 'La Cienega Just Smiled' and 'Rocket Man', Ryan donning huge Elton-style glasses for the latter to add a comic touch to proceedings. Gary Louris of The Jayhawks was another welcome guest on a tour where every night seemed to bring a new surprise in sets that could last as long as three and a half hours.

Ryan was clearly enjoying playing with The (unbilled) Pinkhearts, an experience he described as "really liberating. It's sexy, and it's cool, and I get to spit ice in the air, even. When I write songs now, it doesn't have to be vague. I can write things that don't leave holes open for pedal steel or something. I don't think everybody's gonna like what I'm doing, but I don't care. I like it."

New songs were already shouldering their way into Adams' set – most notably 'Candy Doll', often used as the opener, which harked back to *Exile*-era Stones while 'Desire', trailed from the stage as being inspired by a "cute and cool Canadian girl", was clearly an ode to Alanis you-know-who. The Irving Plaza show was elongated by a three-quarter-hour encore performed entirely solo, the more amazing for the fact that Adams had 'tied one on' the previous night and cancelled media interviews due to the resultant hangover. A 'jilted' reporter from the *New York Post* at least had the compensation of having 'My Winding Wheel', an encore highlight, dedicated to her.

At the end of the day, Ryan Adams had undergone a metamorphosis similar to that enjoyed by David Gray, the British cult singer-songwriter who broke through to the mainstream the previous year with his *White Ladder*. As with Gray's long-time fans, however, there were long-time aficionados who would have much preferred another *Heartbreaker* to the mass appeal of *Gold*. Ryan laughed off such sentiment. "Should I get ready for people to hate me? Hate my guts, say I suck? (But) I never was in their world!"

Singer-songwriter Mike Kemp agreed Adams had now left the alt.country sphere behind. "I don't think he gives a damn about what (former fans) think about him, I think they'll always like him. There are dissenting voices out there somewhere, I think some of that is fuelled by jealousy, as much as anything else. He is the real deal, it would be very easy to write him off as the critic's darling without too much talent if you'd only heard *Gold*, but looking at the output of albums he's put out in a short period of time there's a level of quality there that's no accident.

"Already I'd compare him to Jagger and Richards, and at such a young age that's saying something. OK, he's not a Dylan, he's not a Springsteen, and he's not level with McCartney – yet – but he can be and he could be. And in this day and age, of manufactured pop stars and corporation rock, he's a breath of fresh air."

Bob Harris, too, had noted a certain coolness among the alt.country 'enclave' to Adams' new direction, but believed it was essential for Ryan to progress. "I embrace (this) development. I think this journey that he's taken from alt.country crossing into centre field – by which I don't mean the mainstream, just moving closer into rock – has been fascinating to watch. The people who liked *Strangers Almanac* are going to go with him. The people who didn't like it aren't going to be there anyway. He's going to acquire a whole new audience from the rock side which is potentially obviously much bigger if he wants to explore it – but in terms of leaving people behind (people with narrow minds) are the best people to have left behind."

Even Ryan Adams himself had to admit he'd exceeded his own expectations. "I was afraid (*Gold*) wouldn't be as good as *Heartbreaker*, (which) is fucking *rad*. It's horribly sad. I listened to it the other night and I almost couldn't believe I'd made it." With *Gold*, he'd "dropped the sadness factor . . . I used lethargy, really, more than sadness. I wanted to make somebody feel sentimental just by the melody . . . maybe like how The Smiths' records feel."

For the first time in his life, Ryan Adams could claim that personal stability and commercial success were running hand in glove.

9

No One-Man Band

RYAN ADAMS WAS rapidly making Britain something of a stronghold. *Gold* was released on September 24 and entered the UK charts at 20 in the first week of October. By the middle of the month it had sold 30,000 copies nationwide – "less than Kylie Minogue," as one waggish commentator observed, "but more than Victoria Beckham." The following six months would see it ship over 100,000 copies to record shops and be certified gold.

An eight-date British/Irish tour set up for October opened on the 17th at the Shepherds Bush Empire, a standing downstairs/sitting upstairs venue once used by the BBC for its *In Concert* programmes. It somehow has the kind of atmosphere that the House of Blues spends so much money trying to obtain. Significantly, it was full right up to the third (highest) balcony.

The Pinkhearts, now apparently re-named LAX (the international identity code of Los Angeles International Airport), consisted of a combination of talents – and it needed to be to attempt the wide range of Adams' output. As ever, no Whiskeytown songs would find themselves in the set, the majority coming from *Gold* alongside a few *Heartbreaker* highlights and some new songs, not to mention his Grammy-nominated Hank Williams tribute, 'Lovesick Blues', fuelled by Bucky Baxter's high-octane steel guitar licks.

It was Baxter who challenged him, on that very stage, to busk a new song that included the words 'Maritime' and 'Chesapeake'. The result, a short acoustic ditty with organ and drums, was an unrehearsed exercise which, in the words of one reviewer "demonstrated Adams' adaptable songwriting talent, and also the fact that musicians don't make good comedians."

Adams' post-song comment ran something along the lines of:

"They ought to book me on *Sesame Street* – as long as they did one where you could cuss." The Rolling Stones-y raunch of 'Tina Toledo's Street Walking Blues' featured a specific tip of the hat to 'Can't You Hear Me Knocking' as the guitarists traded extended jazzy solos over a two-chord vamp.

He ended with a solo encore mini-set which had the crowd "shushing" each other so as not to miss the action. "Let's play for fuckin' *ever*!" he yelled, to much appreciative applause. One dissenter sitting on his hands was *The (*London*) Times*'s David Sinclair who, having dubbed him 'Rocky Bodacious', believed his "disorganised encores" sounded "increasingly like a busker on the Northern (Underground) Line." Yet while Ryan had taken to the piano for 'The Bar Is A Beautiful Place', there'd still been no place for 'Goodnight, Hollywood Blvd' and 'La Cienega Just Smiled' in the eight-song encore to a two-hour show for which the touts outside had been demanding (and getting) £75 a ticket.

But just as the public were responding in numbers, the British press, with their notorious 'build 'em up and knock 'em down' philosophy, were lining up behind Sinclair to take pot-shots at their one-time blue-eyed boy. *The Independent* newspaper's Fiona Sturges clearly preferred her Adams solo and unadorned. "His backing band continue in their efforts to turn the evening into a stadium rock event circa 1985," she complained. "Let's hope he leaves them at home next time." The *Evening Standard*'s Max Bell, a previous convert, concurred, suggesting LAX "lived up to their name" (ie, lax) and that he'd "started to come across all rock'n'roll, like Springsteen on a bender." (Saxophonist Leo Green, possibly the catalyst for the comparison, was a notable absentee from the shows that followed.)

The *New Musical Express*, so often an Adams champion, also surprisingly joined the backlash. Nial O'Keeffe rated the encore "profoundly tedious, confirming fears that Adams has mutated into a mature, professional artiste, barely recognisable from the endearing hellraiser of old." And while Adams was now "a happier and more stable person than he's ever been, the truth is that, as far as great music is concerned, redemption ain't always what it's cracked up to be."

Four days later, after a brief stop at TV centre for a *Later With Jools Holland*, Ryan Adams found a critic who still believed. Former *Sounds* stringer Mick Middles, now of *Classic Rock* magazine, witnessed the performance at the Manchester Academy and was content to burn his superlatives at both ends. "The last time I saw an emergent singer-songwriter boasting such scope and precocity was in 1975, and his name was Bruce – so who knows what the future holds?" he slavered.

On to Glasgow, where according to student newspaper *Vibe*, Ryan was "obviously drunk when he came on stage . . . the crowd was plastered too and obviously up for anything." Spontaneity was obviously the order of the day at Queen Margaret University, and Ryan even took to the drums while inviting an audience member to murder the Stooges' 'Search And Destroy'.

Beth Orton and Johnny Cash covers were also essayed in an evening the anonymous reviewer claimed was "perhaps the best gig I've ever been to. Adams is the figurehead for all the country rock fans who are too young to have seen their heroes at the peak of their careers (or alive) and tonight it was clear to see he is perfectly entitled to steal their crowns." A bootleg tends to back up this over-the-top assertion, the audience participation on 'My Winding Wheel' a truly moving experience.

The horror of September 11 (or 9/11, as the Americans colloquially term it) had caused problems for Ryan attempting to promote the album. The choice of a first single, 'New York, New York', not only meant delaying the original October 22 release date but considering the shooting of an alternative video. Amazingly, he'd never made a promo clip of any kind before this one, and thus had never lip-synched to camera. But he decided that the film, completed four days before the atrocity, was "the city as we knew it and saw it. We decided to stay with this video because it was what it was. If people don't want to show the video or don't like it, I understand. We're not pushing it or anything, saying, 'Here's the video with the towers.' It's just out there." Certainly, the result bordered on the poignant, its final shot showing Ryan turning and looking across the Hudson River to the Twin Towers themselves.

September 11 and the bombings in Afghanistan that followed also caused many Americans to cancel their trips abroad, in fear of reprisals. That example was followed by a good number of musicians, but Ryan went ahead with his European tour – a decision all the more praiseworthy in the light of both a hand injury and a hitherto unrevealed fear of flying. "I went two whole years without being able to get on a plane. It's still not easy. I need a window seat, and I will not get on anything that has a propeller. But the band talked about it, and we decided that we didn't want this to stop us from doing what we would have done naturally."

The injury, a broken bone in his right (strumming) hand, had been occasioned the previous weekend at Los Angeles' House of Blues. Everyone was remaining tight-lipped about exactly what had taken place, though thoughts of the smashed Whiskeytown Firebird came to mind. Plan A was for Ryan to soldier on with the aid of painkillers, but steel/acoustic guitarist Bucky Baxter, was ready to plug in and rock out (Plan B) if and when called upon.

Pain and discomfort aside, the tedium of the promotional merry-go-round affected Adams as much as any musician – and, at the children's Saturday morning TV show *CD:UK* in November he got the last laugh on the machine. Also on the show was Sir Paul McCartney, which meant that Adams and crew were inevitably some distance from the centre of attention. So, for a laugh, he and bassist Billy Mercer decided to adopt each other's personalities during what was a by-now routine lip-synch to a playback.

"We just changed identities for the day," Adams later admitted. "We switched wallets and money and caps. Billy also wore the cast (on his hand). Nobody knew the difference." Well, except for one person – and an ex-Beatle at that! "Paul McCartney came up to me afterwards," said a shame-faced Mercer, "and said, '*You're* not Ryan Adams.' I've got no idea how he knew we had made a switch. I also felt kinda bad because a couple of people asked me for autographs, so they think they have Ryan's autograph when they have mine. But I did get a chance to meet Paul McCartney, so it was cool."

The identity switch was not made for a show at London's Astoria venue on November 20 to celebrate the belated release of 'New

York, New York'. Indeed, the night's entertainment would find Ryan in solo mode supporting his band-backed self with a 30 minute acoustic set playing his songs on guitar and piano – a move that won the approval of a sold-out house and all the more impressive in view of his hand. Most of *Gold* was featured as well as the now obligatory cover of Elton John's 'Rocket Man', the Stones' 'Brown Sugar' and The Ramones' 'I Don't Wanna Work' – plus a self-penned song so new the band had never heard of it!

After a 20-minute break, the full band returned to play for over two hours, one wag in the audience greeting this reappearance with the mock taunt of "Judas!" The prescribed answer, "I don't believe you, you're a *liar*," came back across the monitors in imitation of the famous exchange in 1966 between Bob Dylan and a fan irate at his 'electrification'.

One newspaper gossip columnist spotted politician Geoff Hoon among the crowd "bopping with friends". When last spied at a London show, watching Scots Del Amitri, Hoon had been a mere Labour Party politico: now, having shaved off his facial hair and risen to the rank of Defence Secretary, he was clearly a suitable case for the spotlight.

A post-gig party saw the star of the show getting into more than friendly conversation with British 'new folk' singer Beth Orton. The pair had got together on his previous visit to London ('The Bar Is A Beautiful Place' having been dedicated to her from the stage) and, since the highly rated singer who was busy recording her comeback album after a period in the pop wilderness and her label boss Jeff Barrett was an Adams fan, a collaboration of some kind was clearly on the cards.

The song would be 'Concrete Sky', which when issued as a single in July 2002 became her first release in three years. The fact that the song to which Ryan contributed vocals was written by ex-Smiths guitarist Johnny Marr was surely a bonus. A second collaboration, 'This One's Gonna Bruise', surfaced on the album *Daybreaker*. "It was a song that I wrote that she kind of tweaked a little bit, and it's just me on acoustic guitar and her singing." (Two more Orton compositions, 'Carmella' and 'God Song', feature Adams instrumentally.)

The infatuation even extended to rehearsing a stage cover version of 'The Sweetest Decline', a song from her 1999 Mercury Award-winning album *Central Reservation.* The Glasgow show featured an acoustic version, though it was more usually played with the band. Ryan called Beth from the Manchester stage on his mobile phone so she could enjoy the performance – and she seemingly enjoyed it so much that, on the 29th at the Gotta Kallare in Stockholm, she came onstage to sing the song to Adams' piano accompaniment. The lyrics, 'What are regrets?/They're just lessons we haven't learned yet' and 'You can't pin this butterfly down' clearly struck chords.

As well as all this, and touring Scandinavia together, they cut a ballad version of The Stones' 'Brown Sugar' (as per the encore) to be released as a cover-mounted CD with December's *Uncut* magazine. The film, music and culture glossy had long been a champion of Adams, their Nigel Williamson being allowed unrivalled access to the star both in Britain and on home turf. The CD was one of two on offer, and Ryan's presence meant *Volume 1* (also featuring The Charlatans and Kelly Jones of The Stereophonics) sold out the quicker.

Whiskeytown's last will and testament, *Pneumonia,* had finally made its appearance some five months before *Gold* in May. While Ryan, Caitlin and Mike Daly had discussed reuniting for a show or two to celebrate its eventual release they decided against it, so as not to give fans the "wrong impression" as to their (lack of) future together. After the two-year delay triggered by the merger of Universal and PolyGram, the album's release was greeted with little real fanfare. And that was reflected in the initial sales figures. The set débuted on the *Billboard* pop chart at number 158 in the June 9 issue, dropping off the chart the next week.

An interesting sidelight on the *Pneumonia* project surfaced in August 2001 when Ryan and James Iha (who, it will be remembered, had sessioned on the album) were alleged to have got together with Lemonhead-in-chief Evan Dando and ex-Hole bassist Melissa Auf Der Maur to form a kind of alternative supergroup.

According to a spokesperson for Iha's label, Scratchie Records, they were to record an album together that autumn at Stratosphere

Sound, the new Manhattan recording studio jointly owned by Iha, Fountains Of Wayne guitarist Adam Schlesinger and Andy Chase, with whom Schlesinger played in a band called Ivy. This would then be released on Lost Highway Records under the name of The Virgins (some reports stated Fucking Virgins). If it happened, it never surfaced, though some live jamming between Ryan, James Iha and some other unknown players was said to have taken place late one night after a show played in Chicago. Perhaps it was this that inspired some alcohol-fuelled after-hours flights of fancy.

Though the collapse of Iha's band The Smashing Pumpkins had certainly left him with time on his hands (he'd recorded a 1998 solo album *Let It Come Down*, with assistance from Whiskeytown alumni Greg Leisz and John Ginty, produced by Jim Scott), that wasn't a problem from which Ryan Adams was likely to suffer. *Gold* had garnered incredible reviews and had been named one of the best albums of the year by very many reviewers on both sides of the Atlantic. In Britain, *Gold* had proved to be the first alt.country album to reach the mainstream Top 20, and in deference Ryan was included on a compilation called *Beyond Nashville* which also named a series of concerts at London's Barbican Centre featuring Giant Sand, Steve Earle and other well-known names.

By this point, and with those three Grammy nominations under his belt, Ryan Adams was in danger of becoming the household name his Canadian near-namesake had once been. He'd even found time to record a duet with a Swedish singer, Ida Kristin. 'Love Is How We Stay Alive' was scheduled to appear on her summer 2001 album, *Stumble* (V2 Records), though the Scandinavian songbird failed to benefit from more than a flash of the Adams publicity spotlight.

Ryan received what he would doubtless consider one of the ultimate compliments when *Uncut*'s Nigel Williamson brought him into a review of Mick Jagger's solo album, suggesting the Stones singer had been "checking out Whiskeytown and other contemporary alt.country heroes." Ironically, the very next month Adams was slated to share the cover of *Mojo* with a period shot of the Glimmer Twins (albeit in an inset pic, labelled 'Meet the New

Boss'). But the death of George Harrison on press day bumped all three – Adams, Jagger and Richards – off . . . so to speak.

As someone who derived inspiration from his many affairs, the spotlight was on Ryan Adams' love life. And he began 2002 in a publicly acknowledged relationship with singer-songwriter Leona Naess. (What is it with these Scandinavians?) Born in Norway but raised in London, she had released two albums on MCA, 2000's acoustic *Comatised* and the just-released *I Tried To Rock You But You Only Roll.*

Having earned pocket money as a Calvin Klein model, Naess was as easy on the eye as the ear, and was signed up as Adams' support act for a string of dates starting in Los Angeles in late February. She'd played four shows with him acoustically in the pre-Christmas period, accompanied by a guitarist.

Adams was initially guarded about mentioning his new girlfriend's identity in interviews, mindful of Amy Lombardi's hate mail. But he soon relented. "Go ahead and use her name," he said, shrugging. "As soon as we start doing shows together, I'm sure everyone will realise what's going on." As for their musical compatibility, the description of Leona by one entranced critic – "her voice is Edie Brickell meets Suzanne Vega, her songs are Beth Orton meets Fiona Apple, and her looks are Alanis meets Julianna Margulies . . . it's a near-perfect combination" – says it all. Naess herself confessed to a liking for the Eighties pop of Madness, The Cure and Blondie that added a slightly tacky edge to proceedings – something of which Ryan was also fond.

Naess was reputedly the inspiration for a new song, 'World War 24', written in February 2002 and played live the following day. Antique shops, playing chess and, appropriately, London featured in the stream of consciousness lyrics of a song that would surprisingly fail to appear on his *Demolition* demos collection released later in the year.

Naess and Adams would soon be seen in each other's company on the video for 'Answering Bell'. If Bryan Ferry, for one, had come to rue the day he used a current girlfriend in a promotional clip – Jerry Hall having left him for Mick Jagger after her strutting'n'howling in 'Let's Stick Together' – then Adams hedged his bets by padding out the venture with a big (and star-studded) cast. Shot on New York's Long Island, the plot was "a tripped-out version of *The Wizard Of Oz*", with bassist Billy Mercer starring as the Scarecrow, Counting Crow Adam Duritz (backing vocalist on the track) as the Lion and Elton John as the Wizard dressed high-camp style in purple cape and holding a sceptre. This latter was quite a coup given that Elton dislikes appearing in his own videos, having recently employed Robert Downey Jr to stand in for him.

There could have been yet another familiar face on view, as Ryan had invited Bryan Adams (with a B, note!) to appear when they ran into each other just before Christmas at a hotel where staff had apparently got confused by their names and worried they were about to book the same person in twice! The story sounds rather like Ryan's publicity machine having a seasonal laugh at the gullible press's expense – but in the mad world of Ryan Adams you never could tell.

Ironically Elton, who waves his wand to bless the loving couple's video union, had proved quite the agony aunt for Ryan in providing advice about affairs of the heart. "It sounds weird," said Adams, "but he's a bit like an older brother looking after me . . . he's really good at pep-talking about chick issues. Maybe it's because he has that whole relationship with David (Furnish, Elton's partner) or something. I get a lot of support from him."

'Answering Bell' was released in March 2002 as *Gold* passed the 100,000-copy sales mark in Britain and thus lived up to its name. The single included not only the video in CD-ROM form but two tracks that were only previously available on the 20,000 limited edition first UK pressing of its parent – 'The Bar Is A Beautiful Place' and 'Sweet Black Magic'. There was also to be a limited edition 'live hits' single featuring live versions of 'Answering Bell', 'New York, New York' and 'To Be Young' plus the CD-ROM video of 'New York, New York' for the delectation of PC-equipped fans.

The previous month had seen Ryan follow in the footsteps of The Beatles and play a show for his long-time champion, the British rock weekly *New Musical Express*. True, the days had long gone when the Poll Winners Party thrown by the *NME* could put on a bill at Wembley Pool (now Arena) with the Fab Four as its heart for four consecutive years – but, on the plus side, the publication was approaching its 50th anniversary with the avowed intention of putting itself back on the map as trendsetters in matters musical. The bill of Travis, Ryan and Starsailor at London's Astoria was perhaps prematurely hailed as Gig of the Year on the cover of the paper before it had even happened. (Adams had also been nominated in the *NME*/Carling Awards for the Best Solo Artist category.)

Starsailor front man James Walsh was a fan, having first encountered Ryan at one of his two Lyric Theatre, Hammersmith, shows nearly a year previously and been impressed by what he'd heard and seen. "It was one of those shows you'll remember forever," he gushed in a three-way interview – undoubtedly conducted separately – that also included Travis' Fran Healy. "It was really organic, natural-sounding, it sounded effortless. His songs are instantly recognisable – the warmth of it all."

And when it came to the big night, *Dotmusic* website's reviewer Chris Heath described the scene evocatively: "Who is this great white hope of rock'n'roll on whom we've digested so many column inches? Apparently that's him, the shabby tramp figure that staggers on in a charity show suit and loudly vulgar tie. You wonder if this is the wrong gig, or you've simply gatecrashed the soundcheck as the stage is still lit and he's taping lyrics to the floor, apologising for the delay. By the end of the evening this behaviour looks frankly normal."

The multi-band bill made it scarcely worth Ryan bringing his backing musicians with him, so he spiced up a solo performance with two female string players – consciously or otherwise invoking the ghost of Whiskeytown. Not that many of the liggers at the *NME*/Carling Awards Show (as it was grandly billed) seemed to be bothered: most of them probably thought Whiskeytown was some kind of cocktail. The general hubbub was such that Ryan had to call for hush – "Don't mind me, I'm just playin' a fuckin' song!" – after a brusque, opening 'To Be Young' had failed to still the crowd.

A new song to all those present, the cello-augmented, Leona Naess-inspired 'World War 24', elicited the comment, "It's not great, but it'll do", while another newcomer, a piano ballad, was not accorded an official title but featured James Walsh's return to the stage in a backing vocal capacity – backing in more than one respect, as he shyly turned away from the audience. According to what could be heard of the between-song chat, the pair had co-written it, but you wouldn't swear to the fact. Three other songs were being road-tested on the night, though if their writer sought to evaluate their potential by the relative level of applause then he would have been disappointed.

As he vacated the stage for "that guy Travis", Adams hadn't made too many new converts among the chattering classes, but could reflect on a job well done in confirming his status among believers as an original. As reviewer Chris Heath put it, "On a bill where he's sandwiched between such mediocrity, Adams' unstructured insanity is light relief."

Ryan had repaid the debt to the *NME* for services rendered. He would return later in the month to attend another industry junket, the Brit Awards, where he was nominated in the Best International Male category alongside the mighty Bob Dylan – 62 this year and still on his Never-Ending Tour – rap icon Dr Dre and eventual winner Shaggy. He was not to succeed Eminem as holder of an award Prince (or his symbol) had dominated with four wins in the last decade, but on the plus side there were few there who had to be reminded of who he was, or have him differentiated from his Canadian near-namesake.

The Brits were all very well, but the 44th annual Grammy Awards was the real deal. All eyes were on U2 with eight nominations, but Ryan was up for Best Male Rock Vocal Performance ('New York, New York', against Eric Clapton, Dylan, Lenny Kravitz and John Mellencamp); Best Rock Album (*Gold*, against Aerosmith, PJ Harvey, Linkin Park and U2); and Best Male Country Vocal Performance ('Lovesick Blues', against Johnny Cash, Lyle Lovett, Tim McGraw, Willie Nelson and Ralph Stanley from the *O Brother, Where Art Thou?* soundtrack). Alicia Keys, U2 and *O Brother* were to be multiple winners at the Staples Center in

Los Angeles, though the atmosphere was muted in the aftermath of September 11.

Playing the South By Southwest festival had become something of a tradition for Adams – and 2002 in Austin saw him attempt to repeat the previous triumphs by pushing the envelope. This time, in the company of The Pinkhearts, he rampaged through a set of previously unheard songs that reportedly merged the looseness of Crazy Horse and the raunch of the Stones. "Those guys are loud as (Led) Zeppelin," he claimed – and few who witnessed the set would disagree, though the audience seemed split 50-50 as to whether they actually approved of what they were hearing. (Happily, label-mate Lucinda Williams was able to soothe the furrowed brows of those who didn't.)

Ryan and The Pinkhearts played a sub-45 minute set, as SXSW rules dictated (only The Black Crowes succeeded in defying this edict), but given that songs like 'I Don't Want To Work' strained to reach the 90-second mark this was no problem. "It's sort of like bleeding-heart rock'n'roll," he explained of this music, "kind of like skateboarding: it just is what it is. It's not really like, 'Hey, look how serious I am', but a totally off-the-cuff rock'n'roll record." The session, featuring 'Starting To Hurt', 'Gimmie A Sign' and 'Song For Keith' (dedicated, of course, to the chief Stone, and aptly featuring long-time Rolling Stones saxophonist Bobby Keys), came together in the familiar surroundings of Nashville's Woodland Studios.

His record label certainly seemed happy to indulge him, though there was no immediate prospect of the as-yet-untitled Ryan/ Pinkhearts album being released. "It's crazy," label boss Luke Lewis said. "He writes a song or two every day. He's got a quick, busy mind. It's a stretch to call anybody a genius, but he's certainly got some of it in him." The Pinkhearts effort had been produced by Dave Domanich (of Lenny Kravitz renown) rather than Ethan Johns. "Ryan and I weren't in agreement about much on that one," shrugged a clearly unimpressed Johns, before adding diplomatically, "I think Ry had a good time . . ."

There had, indeed, been something lost as well as something gained, as Mike Kemp muses. "I have to admit, as an artist, that I prefer his Whiskeytown stuff, and not because of the way the songs are performed. I think there was an emotional purity about that, that songwriting, that was written by this young man with completely clear eyes, a child-like view of the world. Now it's lost forever – and that's nothing to do with Whiskeytown the band or Ryan Adams' solo career, it's just to do with growing up. Bruce Springsteen is never gonna write *Born To Run* again – you *can't* write that again. That wasn't written with his head, that was written with his heart."

The shark who had to "move forwards or die" was certainly making progress on a number of fronts. But did he have it in him to produce the killer album that would turn *Gold* into platinum? More to the point, is that what he wanted to do?

10

Demolition And Construction

SO WHAT WAS the difference between Ryan Adams the Whiskeytown figurehead and the superstar singer-songwriter that had emerged? Broader shoulders, it seemed. "I had a rough time being a rock personality at 21," he admitted as the new millennium hit its stride. "As you get older, I think your survival muscles get bigger. You are able to fend off more self-deprecating feelings and inadequacies that make you want to go out and get trashed. You see enough people letting their addictions get ahead of them or becoming disenchanted with their life because things aren't going their way that you realise screwing up doesn't seem to be an answer any longer."

That view contrasted with many of his fans who, if bulletin-board posts were anything to go by, had used his example to justify not growing up. That said, he was well on his way to justifying the faith of those who'd backed him all along – like Mark Williams who, you'll remember, signed the then little-known Whiskeytown while at Outpost. Now an A&R executive with Interscope/Geffen/A&M, he likens Ryan to Neil Young in terms of his wide-ranging output. "I see Ryan in very much a similar context. Neil could go and make a Crazy Horse record with a rock band or he could go and make *Comes A Time* or *Harvest*, a more traditional, folk-based kind of a record – or he could make more experimental records. "I have no doubt he's going to evolve and make fantastic records over a long career."

Singer-songwriter Mike Kemp also favoured a Young comparison, but had a further telling angle to add. "Neil Young releases everything he records, and it's up to his fans to take it or leave it. You know with Neil Young that you're gonna buy his album, you're gonna get twelve tracks: eight are gonna be fillers, and four are gonna be awesome, and that's great.

"With Springsteen, you're going to buy twelve tracks of which eleven are gonna be awesome and you might have one you don't particularly like. Neil Young gives you an album a year, and Springsteen gives you one album every five years. I prefer Springsteen's work, but as a fan I'd rather have Neil Young because one man's meat is another man's poison you know. I think Ryan Adams is in that school of thought."

Bob Harris was also happy. "It's a particular pleasure I feel that people are coming to my country show on Thursday nights from rock or other areas of music to discover there's loads and loads about Ryan Adams-type country music that resonates with them, they can feel and identify with. Ryan's doing such a great job – unwittingly, he's just following his own individual course. But for people like me he actually assumes more significance than that."

Certainly, the rumour mill was awash with potential releases at the beginning of 2002 – most of those rumours starting with Adams himself. Whatever he did, Ryan insisted he was unlikely to replicate the song-fest that was *Gold*. "After I made this long-form record, I went, 'Well, I never want to do this again, for a long time'," he said. "I want to make an acoustic record . . . much in the vein of something like (Neil Young's) *Harvest* or something that's just brief, about one subject, teeters off a little bit, but it makes those songs more important. You don't have to fish through so much. Brevity is great. I didn't learn the art of wanting to accomplish that until just recently." Working with producers other than Ethan Johns suggested he was interested in taking direction from third parties.

Another possibility, he explained, was a record of opposites. "It would be great if half of my next record is complete, utter dark testifying; the other half is utter flowery, dripping romance. Complete optimism. And complete pessimism. A *Sticky Fingers* of my own. I'm ready for a twelve-song motherfucker of an album that no one can ever touch, ever. Every last note, every last song, you can't touch. And I've got the right band for it. Now it's just time to get in the kitchen and turn the gas on."

But this was all for the future. As 2002 began, at least five albums of widely differing material already appeared to be 'in the can' awaiting release. The first of these, *The Suicide Handbook*, was an acoustic effort which Ryan had taken to calling *Commercial Suicide* as it grew to fill two discs with "21 miserably sad songs. They might have been the follow-up to *Heartbreaker*, but I didn't want to be the bummer king, so I made *Gold* instead. A lot of the songs from that session are about a girl in Hollywood. It was a painful break-up, so I went back to Nashville, lost weight, took too many drugs . . ."

This labour of the heart was begun in December 2000 in Nashville's Javelina studios, and was the album often compared to Dylan's *Blood On The Tracks*, cut and produced solo save for Bucky Baxter's accompaniment and knob-twiddling by Warren Peterson. Six songs from the sessions had made *Gold*, in re-recorded versions, including 'Answering Bell'. These were songs he'd "always loved, but I knew it wasn't a record to follow *Heartbreaker*." (Bucky Baxter, incidentally, identified "a Bruce Springsteen *Nebraska* feel", but agreed it was just too similar to its predecessor to make releasing it a commercial proposition.

But that wasn't all – not by a long chalk! Just three weeks after making *Gold*, his mood had been lifted by seeing Alanis Morissette in concert at Los Angeles' El Rey theatre. "I watched her rocking and went, 'Man, I think I can make another record – and I want to make it in two days. So I did." The result of this rush of inspiration was the suitably titled *48 Hours*.

Recorded and mixed in the time stated at Hollywood's Cello Studios with Ethan Johns tackling the technical side, the result was compared by Ryan to Dylan's *John Wesley Harding* and The Grateful Dead's *Workingman's Dead*, "a country-folk thing with some shitkicking Merle Haggard stuff in there." Typical of the latter was the irrepressible 'Chin Up, Cheer Up' which could even have been George Harrison in his Travelin' Wilburys days. Come to think of it, he once recorded a song called 'Cheer Down'. . . .

Other songs that were recorded and mixed for the album (most of which remain mere titles) include 'Desire', 'Born Yesterday', 'Drunk And Fucked Up', 'So Blue', 'A Song For Carina', 'This One's For The Rose', 'The Walls', 'Chin Up, Cheer Up', 'Oh

Angelyne', 'Little Moon Don't Shine', 'Hallelujah' and 'You're All Gone'. "There is some fantastic music there," Ethan Johns has stated, "but it's in a very rough state. There are eight great cuts and a few that don't quite make it. We cut the record in a weekend."

Then there was another album cut with The Pinkhearts – Messrs Mercer, Pemberton, Rice and Baxter, his road band – in a garage mode. The second session, produced like the first by Dave Domanich, saw them cross town to Javelina. 'Nuclear (Shut Up And Go To Sleep)', 'Tennessee Sucks' and 'Tomorrow' were song titles associated with this later session. "It's really liberating for me to cock my hip to one side and sneer sometimes," Ryan commented on the project. "Sometimes it just feels good to pick up my guitar and be an idiot. It's not Leonard Cohen or Tom Waits," he admitted, "but it rocks." Legend has it that CDs by Sonic Youth, Iggy & The Stooges and Nirvana were propped on the mixing desk like a shrine to cast the appropriate vibrations on proceedings.

Then, in October 2001 just as *Gold* was released, Ryan returned to the grindstone in Stockholm, "one of my all-time favourite cities", where he was touring with Beth Orton to record nine songs at the Nord Studios with three local musicians – guitarist Mikael Nord Andersson, drummer Michael Blair (famous for appearing on Tom Waits' *Rain Dogs*, and who also produced) and cellist Svante Henrysson. Whether Beth appeared on these recordings varied according to which studio keyhole your ear was at. Recorded song titles include 'Madeline', 'Poor Jimmy', 'For Beth' and 'Prison Letter'. It's suspected that the *Uncut* version of 'Brown Sugar' emanated from these sessions.

And the indefatigable Adams was already thinking in terms of future collaborative ventures. He was also keen to pursue a project with Orton, "a fun band where people dance, kind of like Blondie . . . fun rock'n'roll." Then he also wanted to form a punk band "where I can find a crazy singer and be like a Greg Ginn in my own Black Flag." Meanwhile, Ryan paid back a *Gold* favour with a guest appearance on the new Counting Crows album, *Hard Candy*. It featured a song written with Adam Duritz called 'Butterfly In Reverse'.

It seemed he was intent on covering every musical base he could think of, and seemed unwilling to restrict himself to fields he'd already covered. But what of all this music consigned to tape between late 2000 and late 2001? The only way he could see to cope with this was to put out an album combining the best of all of them – and call it *Cut And Paste*. Another joke? It seemed not: the excellent Adams website Supergold received inside information that suggested a 4CD boxed set was planned for release in 2002, three discs of which would later be made available separately. The fourth would only be available in the set.

From the same source came news that Ryan Adams music was being featured on two movie soundtracks, both released in May. The first, the Bart Freundlich-directed road movie *World Traveler*, featured *Heartbreaker*'s 'To Be Young', while *The Rookie* included 'In My Time Of Need' from the same source, though this time an alternative version. An actual screen appearance with Willie came in an advert for Gap clothes, when they duetted on Hank Williams' 'Move It On Over' – but the creation of new music unavailable to fans inspired calls of 'sell-out' from outraged Ryanophiles.

But there had been indications that Ryan Adams wasn't willing to limit himself to matters musical. He'd talked to *NME* in September 2001 of a play, *Sweetheart*, set in a kitchen in New York and a book he aimed to complete "by next spring" entitled *The Bastard Diaries Of Los Angeles*. "It's kind of a dreamscape and self-analysis, me thinking about the world on paper," he elaborated to a British broadsheet. The idea was to compare "the entire world and my entire life to things I saw on Hollywood Boulevard when I was living in a haunted hotel there." The result was, apparently, narrative prose, "like an ongoing poem, but readable like a regular paragraphed book." He compared it to Miller or Kerouac – "but not nearly as good."

How, then, was this different to his confessional songs? "I'll never tire of music," he explained, "but one day it would be nice to sit behind a typewriter and express myself that way. You can't forever be behind a guitar and take yourself remotely seriously."

Painting was also claiming a significant amount of his spare time, and September 2002 would see him confident enough to mount an exhibition at Niagara, a bar in New York's trendy East Village owned by friend and fellow recording artist Jesse Malin (the pair had briefly collaborated three years before as Snow Kobra). Self-deprecatingly titled *R.I.P. PAINTINGS – A Celebration of Crappy Paintings, 2002 By Ryan Adams*, it attracted such luminaries as Marianne Faithfull and Rufus Wainwright, as well as sometime love Leona Naess. The musical soundtrack of the evening ranged from The Clash to Neil Young, with some of Ryan's own unreleased material thrown in. Titles of the individual pictures included *Me On Cocaine*, the weird self-portrait *I Am The Devil*, *Sadness* and *Intrinsic NYC Bowling*.

He certainly wasn't the first rock singer to try his hand at painting – even the mighty Sir Paul McCartney had recently exhibited in his home town of Liverpool – but the feeling was that, like his songs, they provided a daily journal of life in Adams' world. (He'd repay the debt to exhibition host Jesse Malin by producing his first solo album, *The Fine Art of Self Destruction*, due for release in January 2003 by Artemis Records.)

The next musical aim for Ryan Adams was to replicate the adoration received in Britain to his home country – and television was probably the best way to achieve this. Hitching a ride on the coat-tails of a famous fan seemed another effective tactic, so when the Country Music Television channel's *Crossroads* series, designed to explore the common country roots of artists from diverse backgrounds, gave Ryan and Elton John the chance to consummate their mutual admiration in public fashion in early 2002, they jumped at it. The country equivalent of MTV had matched the likes of Lucinda Williams and Elvis Costello, Kid Rock and Hank Williams Jr and ZZ Top and Brooks & Dunn in previous 'experiments'.

Scheduled for taping at the Hammerstein Ballroom in New York City on March 19, the event unexpectedly turned into an Elton solo showcase when illness kept Adams from the stage. CMT had only learned that very afternoon that Ryan would not be able to perform. He came to the venue in the morning and tried to sing during rehearsal but by mid-afternoon it was clear that he wasn't going to get his voice back. A doctor's opinion was sought, and the consensus was that he was not going on.

Elton played the first show alone, calling out Ryan's backing musicians to perform 'La Cienega Just Smiled' and 'Oh My Sweet Carolina' as a tribute to the absent singer. They also accompanied him on the Jim Reeves country classic 'He'll Have To Go' – a song Elton sang solo in English pubs in his early years – and his own 'Rocket Man'.

The scene changed to Nashville for the rescheduled show, which took place in early April before an invited audience in Studio A of the Grand Ole Opry. Though separated by a generation, John (55) and Adams (27) found enough common ground to sustain a two-hour show, collaborating on all the performances. Elton kicked off the night, taking the lead on 'Firecracker', Ryan singing harmony and taking lead on the bridge. He then strapped on an acoustic guitar and stepped up to the mike for 'Mona Lisas And Mad Hatters' from Elton's *Honky Chateau*, an album he described later in the show as a "vibe-y record".

And that's just how it went throughout the night. A beaming Elton introduced his performance of 'La Cienega Just Smiled' as "my favourite song from *Gold*, and that's saying a lot," before Adams reciprocated with 'Daniel'. Next up came 'Oh My Sweet Carolina', the song from *Heartbreaker* that had "inspired me to go back to basics and do the album I did last year."

Answering audience members' questions, Adams named Loretta Lynn his all-time favourite country singer, followed closely by Tammy Wynette. John rattled off a list that included George Strait, Patsy Cline, Vince Gill, Jim Reeves, Merle Haggard, Waylon Jennings and Willie Nelson. He called country music "the most original white music to come out of America."

Soon after, the duo tried 'He'll Have To Go' for size, problems with a teleprompter sadly sabotaging Adams' contribution. But a break to allow technicians the time to fix it gave the assembled musicians the chance to jam on country classics like Johnny Cash's 'I Still Miss Someone' and Jerry Lee Lewis' 'Great Balls Of Fire' – this the only one on which Elton took the lead vocal. Ryan pulled his version of Hank Williams' 'Lovesick Blues' out of the bag before suggesting a couple of Gram Parsons/Burritos faves, 'Ooh Las Vegas' and 'Sin City', further underlining their common grounding in country music.

Bucky Baxter's steel added colour to Elton's 'Tiny Dancer' before 'Rocket Man', rearranged to suit Adams' band, brought proceedings to a close and earned all concerned a deserved ovation.

Meanwhile, Ryan had gigs to play in his pal's homeland, and, thanks to the TV special's rescheduling, less than a week to prepare for them. The short British tour kicked off at Manchester's Apollo on Sunday, April 7, before travelling south to the capital, where the exotically seedy surroundings of the Brixton Empire were to be his temporary home for a two-night stand.

The press was awash with reports that Ryan had recorded a 'solo blues version' of *Is This It?*, the much-praised début album by New York band The Strokes, on a four-track tape recorder. He encouraged the rumours by playing a version of The Strokes' 'Last Nite' after requests from the Manchester crowd, but there's every indication that this was a spur-of-the moment scam the press had refused to let go of.

The capital's ticket touts seemed bemused at the lack of demand at what was a sold-out show (a second date, 10 April, was added), so maybe the powers that be had exactly estimated the level of interest. Certainly the atmosphere inside the faded palace of varieties was expectant. A mix of the sexes, hard drinking, smoking . . . a hubbub of excitement pervading the venue.

Support band Proud Mary were a canny choice to heighten the mood still further. A six-piece who'd clearly paid great attention to their mums' and dads' record collections while still in short trousers, they purveyed a brand of retro-rock somewhere between Free (the tambourine-toting singer), Humble Pie (the semi-acoustic-wielding rhythm guitarist) and The Faces (the studiedly yobbish keyboard player). No surprise, then, that they'd been signed to Noel Gallagher's Sour Mash label – and it was hardly a shock that the Oasis mainman was the surprise special guest on the cover of The Rolling Stones' 'Salt Of The Earth' that closed the Proud Mary set.

The guest appearance, on the eve of Oasis' much-vaunted comeback, caused interval conversation levels to break the decibel barrier. It said much of Ryan Adams that he'd allow such a gauntlet to be thrown down, confident he had his fans where he wanted them. And indeed that proved to be the case, despite an interminable intermission spiced up by the playing of Lou Reed's *Transformer* album – in full.

This was followed by a burst of Elton John – to audible groans from the crowd – and a high-volume burst of Sophie Ellis Bextor's 'Murder On The Dancefloor': the petite indie singer turned dance diva would be the butt of many on-stage cracks in the two hours to come. Adams' top-price tickets were £18.50, while Neil Young, due the following month, could get away with charging £35. Question was: could Ryan Adams amount to more than half a Neil Young?

Well, he certainly did his best. As in Manchester that Sunday, Adams stuck mainly to tracks from *Gold* – highlights including 'Nobody Girl', 'Touch, Feel & Lose' and 'Tina Toledo'. The purpose of the gig was to push his new single 'Answering Bell', the video for which was receiving huge airplay, but its predecessor 'New York, New York' was conspicuous by its absence. Nevertheless, an incendiary opening 'Firecracker' had the audience eating out of his hand.

Adams and his band stumbled on stage looking as if they weren't quite sure where they were. But there was a quiet determination about the man, so much so that he declined to speak until five songs had been delivered, hot and steaming, to the capacity crowd. Somehow the spell was then broken, encouraging him thereafter to crack wilfully corny jokes, light up fags and swig from bottles in a Ronnie Wood parody. He continued the Rolling Stones' theme when 'Tina Toledo', as ever, became the vehicle for an elongated jam session with much strutting and posing. But it wasn't yesterday's Bad Boys of Rock that was on the mind of an audience still boggling from what they had seen at the end of act one . . . and wondering if a repeat performance would be on offer.

Adams had covered Oasis' 'Wonderwall' in previous shows, of course, and it would have been almost too obvious for Gallagher to reappear for this one. Instead, a female cellist and violinist emerged from the wings to accompany a plaintively acoustic Adams, who sung the song straight country style. Was this his way of saying he didn't need Noel? No. This was one boy who knew what his audience wanted, and they got it. Introduced with the words "This is it!", he re-emerged with the Oasis leader for a faithful romp through '(What's The Story) Morning Glory'.

All very well and good, but it left a fair proportion of the departing crowd a trifle confused. As a bloke on the tube was later overheard to say: "Wouldn't you have finished your gig with one of your own songs?"

The early summer found him opening for Alanis Morissette as she promoted her latest album *Under Rug Swept* at such imposing venues as the Verizon Wireless Amphitheater at Irvine, California (where the jaunt kicked off on April 27). Having decided to drop the band, he came on stage in a mood to take no prisoners: at Las Vegas' The Joint, he'd emblazoned 'It's All Good' across the top of his set list. "You have to be either stupid or immensely talented to treat your audience with the level of disdain Adams displayed tonight," reported *Classic Rock* magazine's Rich Wilson, "and tonight he was at his sneering and sarcastic best . . . the belligerence merely adding to the appeal."

As the tour wound up at Portsmouth, Virginia's Harbour Center, he took off to guest on the *Willie Nelson & Friends* TV special. The loudest cheers of that night were reserved for the unholy trio of Ryan, Keith Richards and Hank Williams III with their rendition of The Rolling Stones' 'Dead Flowers'. Adams also played a little reggae with the star of the show, tackling Jimmy Cliff's classic 'The Harder They Come'. This was reprised on *The Late Show With David Letterman* in November 2002, and was scheduled for release on an upcoming Willie Nelson album. (Interestingly, Ryan would repair to Jamaica later that summer to film an episode of MTV's *Music In High Places*. The programme, which aired in the States on 30 August, included footage of him writing a song with ska legend Toots Hibbert of The Maytals.)

Given that, during the salvaging of *Pneumonia*, Ryan had rejected the chance to work with producer Scott Litt of R.E.M., Replacements and Nirvana renown, and partner in Outpost to boot, it was surprising to hear he and Ryan were in the studio recording new material. Rumour had it that Neil Young, Willie Nelson and Hank Williams III (separately or together) were likely to feature –

probably a legacy of the TV special teaming. What was certain, though, was that the 31 songs that had appeared on his live set list since September 2001 had a shot at being considered.

But then came news that the *Cut And Paste* concept had been resurrected, and that Ryan's new album would in fact contain a baker's dozen of previously unreleased demo recordings. Confirmation came in July when he talked to *Rolling Stone*. "Ryan Adams will release *Demolition*, a collection of demo recordings, on September 17," they trumpeted. The album would comprise 13 tracks from several studio sessions over the past two years, some of which were previewed on his official website in the intervening weeks. (The time period would later be narrowed to the ten months from December 2000.)

Demolition, the magazine noted, would be Adams' fourth release in two years. However, he was far from worried about flooding the market: "I don't even care about selling millions of records. I never have. I always wanted to make really cool records."

The new album was débuted at the City Limits Music Festival in Austin in late September, a two-day outdoor event where Emmylou Harris, Wilco and a certain Caitlin Cary would be on the bill. November was spent on a solo tour of the UK, taking in London, Manchester, Edinburgh and Belfast before a couple of nights at Dublin's Olympia Theatre where the 'craic' was always sublime.

If the spirit of Winona Rider had been discernible in *Gold*, then the name and spirit behind *Demolition* was 38-year-old actress and writer Carrie Hamilton. Daughter of comedian Carol Burnett and director-producer Joe Hamilton, she had been close to Ryan but had died in January 2002. (She is the girl in T-shirt and jeans pictured with Ryan on the second page of *Gold*'s CD booklet.)

Though ten years older than Adams, her wild-child past was probably a point of contact. Her teenage substance abuse had led her parents to crusade against drugs, but Hamilton had taken her second chance not only to appear in such television shows as *Fame, Touched By An Angel* and *The X-Files* but turn her mother's memoirs into an acclaimed play, *Hollywood Arms*.

She also had musical leanings, and had written a song with Adams, that appears as track 11 – 'Tomorrow', the most affecting selection on the album. Ryan explained that all the songs he'd chosen "were favourites of a friend of mine who died of cancer. I really loved her, but she's dead. That's what happens." Hence the album dedication "God bless you Carrie Hamilton, wherever you are."

New York Metro magazine was among the first to gain his thoughts on the music. And he was keen to underline the fact that the title was *Demo-lition*, "as in record demo. I wasn't going to release a record this year," he insisted, "because people were getting very tired of me." The minimalist cover of the album, a tape cassette spewing out its innards, left no room for misunderstanding. But there was no doubt that, exactly one year on from *Gold*, his fans were hungry again.

Album opener 'Nuclear' from the *Pinkhearts II* session was written in LA as "a reaction to meeting someone pretty intense . . . it's a song about change." An anthem bidding farewell to the summer, it made an obvious radio-friendly single, though digging deeper beyond a chorus of 'Sentimental geek/Shut up'n go to sleep' didn't really reveal that much.

The lyrics for track two, 'Hallelujah', were finished seconds before the song was recorded for *48 Hours*, which gives it an almost alt.country immediacy. "It's vague, but to the point," said Ryan about a song he wrote "to express a bunch of crap I'd been dealing with." He describes 'Hallelujah' as a "happy accident", and the song has echoes both of Whiskeytown and the joyous *Gold* opener 'Firecracker'.

The Stockholm-recorded 'You Will Always Be The Same' was "the best song ever written about Beth Orton . . . and I've written several." There's more than a touch of Nick Drake to a minimalist ode that states "the world can get fucked up as hell, but you will always mean the same thing to me."

The second of three *48 Hours* cuts, 'Desire', was inspired by "another totally unrequited romance. I really wanted someone's company and attention. In true singer-songwriter bullshit fashion, I recorded the song and she flipped her wig." It's not hard to put Alanis Morissette's name in the frame here as the subject. The song not only shares a title with a famous U2 track but also takes some musical cues from the Irish band, notably the prominent and propulsive bass line.

The first dip into the *Suicide Handbook* comes five songs in, in the shape of the understatedly nasty 'Cry On Demand' – "a mean song I really shouldn't have written . . ." The lyric accuses the unnamed subject of manipulating her emotions, and strongly features Bucky Baxter's vocal. It's tempting to group this with 'She Wants To Play Hearts', which is its musical bookend.

'Starting To Hurt' was inspired by a tale bassist Billy Mercer had told Adams about a woman who jumped off a building in Nashville. "She'd gone up to the top, handed someone her baby and jumped. I had the riff but no words to the song, so I tried to put myself into her character. You can't begin to imagine how she must have been feeling but I tried." *Rolling Stone*'s three-star review rated it "a bouncy slice of mid-tempo cheese that could easily be covered by his doppelgänger Bryan Adams" – the sort of review that makes you want to end it all? In any event, the song, the earliest on the album, lacks a chorus to nail the good work of the verses and ends up sounding like a workaday Del Amitri album track.

Ryan's own favourite song on the album, 'She Wants To Play Hearts', was the second selection from *The Suicide Handbook.* "It's about missing someone and maybe missing myself." Given its immediate post-*Gold* creation, assume it's Winona he's pining after.

Taken from the second Pinkheart sessions, 'Tennessee Sucks' just beat another song on the same subject called 'Saturday Night' to make it to the record. "Tennessee sucks in the summer, worse even than New York. It's not only hot but really humid. Even the beer doesn't help. I wrote it as a gag." Bucky Baxter chips in with "some really fucked-up Paul Simon guitar shit . . .", but the result is at best a throwaway – which, with so much music to choose from, can only be regretted.

A sudden change of geographical location comes with 'Dear Chicago', last of the *Suicide Handbook* selections and a song that by all accounts had originally been intended as the final track on *Heartbreaker.* "It's reflecting on the same thing I always do . . . past romance," said its author. "It's saying I think I've fallen out of love with you and I'm feeling good about it. I'm free. For a second." Two minutes and not much more, this was a track it would have been criminal to keep under wraps.

'Gimme A Sign' from *Pinkhearts I* was "written the day before I met Winona Ryder . . . It was a really good week. I think I wrote it about an American sit-com about vampires called *Dark Shadows*. But I don't remember too well. When The Pinkhearts are around a lot of pot tends to get smoked." Many fans would have preferred 'Candy Doll', a regular set opener near the beginning of the *Gold* tour, to either this or 'Starting To Hurt', but . . .

'Tomorrow', the song co-written with Carrie Hamilton, was created when he was resident at the Hollywood Roosevelt hotel "the day before she was going back to Colorado. It was the last time I was to see Carrie healthy. I'm still going through it and haven't been able to touch it in a song."

After that, the breezy 'Chin Up, Cheer Up', described by Ryan as "bluegrass meets The Smiths – well, kind of!", comes as some kind of antidote. Steel guitarist was Greg Leisz, whose prints had been all over *Pneumonia*. The chord changes are Johnny Marr – "and I'm still studying that guy. I'd been in England just before I wrote it, so it must be about someone unnamed from England who is a better songwriter than I am. You know who I mean." Take a bow Steven Morrissey?

Then comes the album's closer, darker and more melancholy than anything on *Gold*, which returned to Carrie Hamilton. 'Jesus (Don't Touch My Baby)' was written when he first found out his friend was sick. "It was during a Pinkhearts session and I was so upset I kicked them all out of the studio. But I started playing around with the drum machine and this came out. Think I'd been listening to too much Radiohead when I recorded it."

Though not all fans cared for the style, *Rolling Stone*'s reviewer correctly fingered this as a standout song "which sets happy memories of California beaches to moody, atmospheric music, rendering them paranoid. Told to write a song about a silver lining, Adams will always find the cloud." David Bennun of Britain's *Mail On Sunday* assessed the album as "one third excellent, the rest merely accomplished", stating that "having set himself such high standards Ryan now has to be judged by them." Posters on Ryan-related Internet message boards appeared to agree, one typically rating it a "$10 purchase".

But if fan response was muted, Bob Harris regarded the new album as rather more than a step back from the brink of superstardom. He believed "you can see the bridges across (from his influences), which are more defined on this album. I actually love it. This guy is so special as far as I'm concerned. His music catches me in some way and I'm a 100 per cent 'for' person as far as Ryan Adams is concerned. I'm almost in danger on my programmes of overplaying him."

A limited edition single of 'Nuclear' was released in Britain only on September 16 in numbered CD and 7-inch forms. Both formats were deleted on the day of release – a strategy that won Ryan his first Top 40 singles place, albeit at 37 – and featured exclusive new B-sides. The CD single contained a song called 'Blue', while the 7-inch plastic contained the much-vaunted 'Song For Keith'.

Around this time, *Entertainment Weekly* quoted Ryan as saying that, "If people really like *Demolition*, Lost Highway would likely release a boxed set at Christmas time from the 60 or so songs it picked from." Needless to say, no one held their breath . . . The same interview stated he wanted to include Patti Smith guitarist Lenny Kaye, Beck and Marianne Faithfull on his next album – together or separately wasn't stated. (Rumour had it that he and Marianne had recorded together that September in a New York studio, though details were sketchy.)

Hot on the heels of *Demolition* came *Rise Above*, a charity compilation album of Black Flag covers released in October 2002 which gave Ryan's cover of 'Nervous Breakdown' (this version from a Fillmore show in October 2001) another airing.

So what of the future for Ryan Adams? One-time UK press agent Paddy Forwood feels he has "the charisma, the personality and the whole thing to go all the way", though he felt working with a band "with the big sax sound and string vibe didn't do justice to the subtlety and fragility of a lot of his material. The solo stuff, him just standing there on his own in front of a packed house in total silence is amazing, and I feel that's stronger and more impressive than the full rock'n'roll thing, which is fun but doesn't showcase his talent to its fullest."

Fellow singer-songwriter Mike Kemp agrees. "I don't think he's a natural rocker. I see Springsteen as a natural rocker, who happens to excel in an acoustic setting, (but) Ryan Adams is the other way round. I think he's a naturally gifted acoustic, storytelling folk singer, pretty much like Dylan, who happens to be very good – mind you, it's pretty easy to sound good in that band setting when you have people like Bucky Baxter on pedal steel guitar! Don't take away the quality of the people he plays with, that's a very, very big factor."

As for Adams' future career progression, "It's very difficult to see how he will progress. There's a lot of talent there, but is his talent a well that knows no depths? The one charge that could be levelled against him is that he's very generic of what's gone before. But then again, in no way can anyone describe Springsteen as being an original – he's great at putting Chuck Berry riffs with a Rolling Stones guitar sound, a drum sound from The Who and a bit of a 'Dylan-esque' lyric. Bruce found his own voice later in his career; I don't know whether Ryan Adams has got the strength of character to do that. It's nothing to do with talent, he's the master of his own destiny and no one else.

"I can imagine Springsteen, early in his career, playing to a packed-out audience for four hours, going home and sitting in his chair playing his guitar, getting the bits he messed up right – that work ethic. He was a working-class guy who always had to strive for better. Ryan Adams strikes me as someone who is without doubt very talented, but probably doesn't share that same work ethic; things come a bit easy to him. Maybe a lot of that is to do with his natural talent, but I think he'll do just enough rather than push himself. If he pushes himself, you're gonna see something legendary. If he doesn't want to, then all you're gonna see is something great – but at the least it's gonna be great."

Bob Harris would "personally be very surprised if he has a Career Plan, in capital letters, in place or ever has – and I hope to God he never acquires one! Hopefully the development of Ryan Adams music will be this natural process which has been so fantastic to watch. He's incredibly prolific, as we know, and we don't often get artists of Ryan's ability and stature putting out as much material as he does. I think that's brilliant. Thank you very much, I'm glad you're sending us all this material, it's very much appreciated. Let's hope that continues . . ."

Postscript

WHAT OF THE others Ryan Adams left behind in his ascent? The members of Whiskeytown were still very much around, if not quite boasting as high a profile as when their musical orbit had coincided with Ryan's.

Caitlin Cary may not have intended to make music her career, but the pull of the stage clearly wouldn't let go – even if Ryan had. She likened her Whiskeytown experience to "being dragged along by the ears for a few years" or, less painfully, "a relationship with your best friend that turned into a love interest."

Returning to the stage post-*Pneumonia*, she teamed up in 1999 with Lynn Blakey as the two-girl act Dos Chicas, expanding to Tres Chicas the following year with the addition of Tonya Lamm. Their exploration of three-part girl-group harmonies was entertaining if not envelope-expanding.

Her next, slightly more serious effort would be a permanent group, Caitlin Cary & The Come-Ons, which débuted in September 2000 and featured Mike Daly. Mike Santoro, who wrote the bass parts for and played on *Pneumonia*, also became a Come-On, while the Whiskeytown reunion feel was complete in November of that year when Skillet Gilmore – who also plays with Thad Cockrell & The Starlite Country Band – joined the ranks for a three-week British tour. This kicked off at the Borderline, a venue Whiskeytown knew well; indeed Daly had been over earlier in the year accompanying singer-songwriter Chris Mills.

Mindful of the problems she'd observed with Whiskeytown's major-label connections, Cary had gone with a local label, the Chapel Hill, NC-based Yep Roc Records, for her solo début, a five-song EP titled *Waltzie* released in August 2000. Recorded with familiar producer Chris Stamey, *Waltzie* was "the culmination of years of knowing I wanted to do my own record. I needed to figure out if I could be the frontgirl, that was the scary part. I was pretty confident, but with a lot to learn." A certain Ryan Adams also popped up on harmonica, synthesiser and harmony vocals.

A full-length solo album would follow one year later, titled *While You Weren't Looking*. Also on Yep Roc, it was very much a gathering of the usual suspects, Mike Daly co-writing most of the output and a certain R Adams contributing to 'Please Don't Hurry Your Heart'. The latter was an understated song in which Cary's vocal recalled Christine McVie of former Whiskeytown favourites Fleetwood Mac, while Superchunk's Jon Wurster added guitar.

The nearest track to early-period Whiskeytown was perhaps 'Thick Walls Down', with its prominent pedal steel, but this was more than balanced by the ballad 'Sorry' and fiddle-laced 'Pony'.

With Chris Stamey again at the controls, *While You Weren't Looking* was unanimously hailed by the press. "Trekking through love's badlands, her rangy soprano is all hard-won confidence – the sound of an erstwhile second fiddle claiming first chair," said *Entertainment Weekly*, while *No Depression* rated it, "The best recording yet to surface from the remnants of Whiskeytown." *Rolling Stone*'s 3.5-star review said "it demonstrates that, while her bad-boy band mate Ryan Adams was grabbing all the attention as Whiskeytown's frontman, she was writing dreamy folk-pop songs," while *People* magazine concluded she was "worth seeking out". So far, so good . . .

Daly, who in the post-Whiskeytown period had sessioned for a number of acts including the Pernice Brothers and James Iha, was coming up with his own offering, *Letting Go*. "My stuff is song music," he told the *Americana UK* website, "but it's a little more. I guess, if Paul Simon and George Harrison were to hang out with Whiskeytown for a while . . ." His connections with Britain included a friendship with ex-Bible singer Boo Hewerdine, "a good friend", and given his fondness for Travis and Badly Drawn Boy it seemed the UK might see more of him in future.

Meanwhile Ryan's original guitar partner Phil Wandscher had found his niche with a seemingly more amenable singer-songwriter in the shape of Jesse Sykes. The partnership found fruition in April

2002 in the shape of a début album, *Reckless Burning*, produced by Tucker Martine, created with help from some of Seattle's finer musicians and released on the (probably self-funded) Burn Burn Burn label.

Wandscher had relocated to the West Coast after his ejection from Whiskeytown and met his future partner in crime in Seattle's Hattie's Hat bar in 1998. Initially performing as a duo, they duly expanded their line-up to include violinist Anne Marie Ruljancich (Walkabouts), upright bass player Bill Herzog (ex-Neko Case, Joel Phelps and Citizens Utilities) and drummer Kevin Warner (Evangeline). The resulting band was christened Jesse Sykes & The Sweet Hereafter, and found itself sharing bills with the likes of Howe Gelb, Mark Lanagan, Neko Case and The Handsome Family.

Meanwhile came news that Gillan Welch and David Rawlings had bought Woodland Studios where *Strangers Almanac* and *Heartbreaker* had been recorded. The pair's label, Acony Records, bought the studio at 10th and Woodland Street with "no plans to use the renowned studio as a commercial studio for outside projects.

"After our wonderful experience at RCA Studio B (where Welch and Rawlings recorded their Grammy-nominated *Time (The Revelator)*), it was clear that we needed a studio in which we could set up residency. Our methods of recording are unique and a necessary part of our art. We are excited about the space and what it means to the community as well as to our company," said Welch.

No doubt Ryan would be a welcome visitor in the coming months.

Discography

PRE-WHISKEYTOWN RECORDINGS (RELEASED)

Blank Label
Non-Existence/Sonic Issue/JLW
Privately pressed 7-inch; 1991

Patty Duke Syndrome
Texas/History
Blast-O-Platter, BLO-09; 1994 Split 7-inch

WHISKEYTOWN

Albums

Faithless Street (Original Issue)
Midway Park/Drank Like A River/Too Drunk To Dream/What May Seem Like Love/Faithless Street/Mining Town/If He Can't Have You/Black Arrow, Bleeding Heart/Matrimony/Hard Luck Story/Top Dollar/Oklahoma/Revenge (Hidden track)
Mood Food Records MFR 004-2; January 1996

Strangers Almanac
Inn Town/Excuse Me While I Break My Own Heart Tonight/Yesterday's News/16 Days/Everything I Do/Houses On The Hill/Turn Around/Dancing With The Women At The Bar/Waiting To Derail/Avenues/Losering/Somebody Remembers The Rose/Not Home Anymore
Outpost Records OPRD-30005; July 1997

Rural Free Delivery
Take Your Guns To Town/Nervous Breakdown/Tennessee Square/Captain Smith/Macon, Georgia County Line/Pawn Shop Ain't No Place For A Wedding Ring/Oklahoma/Angels Are Messengers From God (Hidden track: Nervous Breakdown)
Mood Food Records MFR 008-2; May 1997

Faithless Street (Augmented Reissue)
Midway Park/Drank Like A River/Too Drunk To Dream/Tennessee Square (Bonus Track)/What May Seem Like Love/Faithless Street/Mining Town/If He Can't Have You/Black Arrow, Bleeding Heart/Matrimony/Excuse Me While I Break My Own Heart Tonight/Desperate Ain't Lonely (Bonus Track)/Hard Luck

Story/Top Dollar/Lo-Fi Tennessee Mountain Angel (For Kathy Poindexter) (Bonus Track)/Revenge/Empty Baseball Park/Here's To The Rest Of The World (Baseball Park Sessions)/16 Days (Baseball Park Sessions)/Yesterday's News (Baseball Park Sessions)/Factory Girl (Baseball Park Sessions)
Outpost Records OPRD-30002; September 1998

Pneumonia
Ballad Of Carol Lynn/Don't Wanna Know Why/Jacksonville Skyline/Reason To Lie/Don't Be Sad/Sit And Listen To The Rain/Under Your Breath/Mirror Mirror/Paper Moon/What The Devil Wanted/Crazy About You/My Hometown/Easy Hearts/Bar Lights (Hidden track: To Be Evil)
Lost Highway Records 088 170 199-2; May 2001

Singles/EPs

Angels EP
Angels Are Messengers From God (aka Faithless Street)/Captain Smith/Tennessee Square/Take Your Guns To Town
Mood Food Records MFR 001-7; May 1995

Theme For A Trucker/My Heart Is Broken
Houses On The Hill/The Strip (aka Dancing With The Women At The Bar)
Bloodshot Records, BS 021; April 1997 Double 7-inch single

In Your Wildest Dreams (Promo EP)
Outpost Records PRO-CD-3008; July 1997

16 Days/The Rain Won't Help You When It's Over/Wither, I'm A Flower
Outpost Records, OPD 22294; 1997

Yesterday's News (radio version)/Yesterday's News (LP version)
Promo CD, Outpost Records, PRO-CD-3014; 1998

Highway 145 (Whiskeytown)/My '63 (Neko Case & The Sadies)
Bloodshot Records, BS 037; 1998 (Split single)

Don't Be Sad
Lost Highway MRNR-02113-2, US, Whiskey CD1, US; May 2001 (Promo CD)

SOLO

Albums

Heartbreaker
(Argument With David Rawlings Concerning Morrissey)/To Be Young (Is To Be Sad, Is To Be High)/My Winding Wheel/AMY/Oh My Sweet Carolina/Bartering Lines/Call Me On Your Way Back Home/Damn, Sam (I Love A Woman That Rains)/Come Pick Me Up/To Be The One/Why Do They Leave?/Shakedown On 9th Street/Don't Ask For The Water/In My Time Of Need/Sweet Lil Gal (23rd/1st)
Bloodshot Records BS 071; September 2000

Gold
New York, New York/Firecracker/Answering Bell/La Cienega Just Smiled/The Rescue Blues/Somehow, Someday/When The Stars Go Blue/Nobody Girl/SYLVIA PLATH/Enemy Fire/Gonna Make You Love Me/Wild Flowers/Harder Now That It's Over/Touch, Feel & Lose/Tina Toledo's Street Walkin' Blues/Goodnight, Hollywood Blvd.
Lost Highway Records 088 170 235-2; September 2001
(Original pressings came with a limited edition five-song disc: Rosalie Come And Go/The Fools We Are As Men/Sweet Black Magic/The Bar Is A Beautiful Place/Cannonball Days)

Demolition
Nuclear/Hallelujah/You Will Always Be The Same/Desire/Cry On Demand/Starting To Hurt/She Wants To Play Hearts/Tennessee Sucks/Dear Chicago/Gimme A Sign/Tomorrow/Chin Up, Cheer Up/Jesus (Don't Touch My Baby)
Lost Highway Records 170 333-2; September 2002

Singles

New York, New York/Mara Lisa/From Me To You/New York, New York (Video)
Lost Highway Records 2712232; November 2001

Answering Bell/New York, New York/To Be Young/New York, New York (video)
Lost Highway Records 172 223-2; April 2002
Answering Bell/The Bar Is A Beautiful Place/Sweet Black Magic/Answering Bell (video)
Lost Highway Records 172 237-2; April 2002

Nuclear/Blue
Lost Highway Records 172 259-2 ; September 2002 (UK only)

Nuclear/Song For Keith
Lost Highway Records; September 2002 (Numbered, 7-inch single) (UK only)

GUEST APPEARANCES, SOUNDTRACKS AND COMPILATIONS

Timeless (Hank Williams Tribute)
Lost Highway UICM1016; October 2001
Ryan covers 'Lovesick Blues'

Return Of The Grievous Angel – A Tribute To Gram Parsons
Almo Records ALMCD66; June 1999
Whiskeytown covers 'A Song For You'

Down To The Promised Land: 5 Years Of Bloodshot Records
Bloodshot Records; May 2000
Ryan plays 'Monday Night'

Poor Little Knitter On The Road – A Tribute To The Knitters
Bloodshot; October 1999
Whiskeytown plays 'Silver Wings'

Exposed Roots – The Best Of Alt.Country
K- Tel Records number unknown
Whiskeytown covers 'Nervous Breakdown'

On The Mountain 4
KMTT 103.7 radio; date unknown
Whiskeytown plays live-in-studio '16 Days'

Car Songs
Bloodshot Records, 1998
Whiskeytown plays 'Highway 145' (Split 7-inch with the Volebeats)

The Tom T Hall Project
Sire Records; October 1998
Whiskeytown covers 'I Hope It Rains At My Funeral'

The Garden Place – Songs for Our Friends
Yep Roc Records; September 1998
Whiskeytown plays 'Me And My Ticket'

Hope Floats Soundtrack
Capital Records; April 1998
Whiskeytown plays 'Wither, I'm A Flower'

Revival 2: Kuzu And Hollerin' Contest
Yep Roc Records; October 1997
Whiskeytown plays a cover of Eric B and Rakim's 'Busted'

The End Of Violence Soundtrack
Outpost Records; September 1997
Whiskeytown plays 'Theme For A Trucker'

Revival 1: Brunswick Stew And Pig Pickin'
Yep Roc Records; March 1997
Whiskeytown plays 'Take Your Guns To Town'

Straight Outta Boone Country
Bloodshot Records BS 019; March 1997
Whiskeytown covers 'Bottom Of The Glass' by Moon Mullican

Tower Of Power
Cred Factory Records; 1997
Ryan plays 'The Great Divide'

Who The Hell? – A Tribute To Richard Hell
Cred Factory Records, CRED 003; 1995
Whiskeytown covers 'Blank Generation'

The Rookie
Hollywood Records; March 2002
Ryan plays an alternative version of 'In My Time Of Need'

UNCUT – Gimme Shelter Vol 1
January 2002
Free CD of Rolling Stones' covers with British music magazine included a duet of Ryan with Beth Orton covering 'Brown Sugar'

GUEST APPEARANCES

Caitlin Cary
Waltzie
Yep Roc Records; August 2000
Ryan sings, plays harmonica, and synthesiser

Bellvue
To Be Somebody
Released August 2001
Ryan Adams on harmony vocals

Ida Kristin
Stumble
V2 Music; August 2001
Ryan Adams on background vocals

Caitlin Cary
While You Weren't Looking
Yep Roc Records CD YEP 2029; March 2002
Ryan Adams on duet vocals

Counting Crows
Hard Candy
Geffen Records; July 2002
Ryan on backing vocals

Beth Orton
Daybreaker
Heavenly Records; July 2002
Ryan Adams on harmony and background vocals, guitar and bass

Alejandro Escovedo
A Man Under The Influence
Bloodshot Records, BS 021; April 2001
Ryan Adams on harmony and background vocals

Lucinda Williams
Essence
Lost Highway; July 2001
Ryan Adams on guitar

Stateside
Twice As Gone
Disgraceland Records; July 2001
Ryan Adams on background vocals

Willie Nelson & Friends
Stars & Guitars
Lost Highway Records: November 2002
Ryan duets on 'Dead Flowers' and 'The Harder They Come'

Website Guide

Official and label website

www.ryan-adams.com
www.losthighwayrecords.com

Good info-based sites

www.megasuperiorgold.com
www.answeringbell.com

Long-standing Whiskeytown/RA fan sites

www.losering.com
www.ryanadamsmusic.com

Online fanzine

www.ohmysweetcarolina.com

Useful alt.country-related sites

www.insurgentcountry.com
www.nodepression.net
www.americana-uk.com
http://www.bobharris.org